Frances Partridge was born in Bedford Square, Bloomsbury, in 1900, one of six children of an architect. She was educated at Newnham College, Cambridge, where she read English and Moral Sciences. In 1933 she married Ralph Partridge, who died in 1960. In addition to translating many books from French and Spanish and helping her husband to edit *The Greville Memoirs*, she is the author of six other published volumes of diaries: *Memories*, *A Pacifist's War*, *Everything to Lose*, *Other People*, *Good Company* and *Life Regained*.

HANGING ON

DIARIES
December 1960 – August 1963

Frances Partridge

A PHOENIX GIANT PAPERBACK

First published in Great Britain
by William Collins Sons and Co. Ltd. in 1990
This paperback edition published in 1998
by Phoenix, a division of Orion Books Ltd,
Orion House, 5 Upper St Martin's Lane,
London WC2H 9EA

A CIP catalogue record for this book is available
from the British Library.

ISBN: 0 75380 108 6

Printed and bound in Great Britain by
Butler & Tanner Ltd, Frome and London

List of Illustrations

Foreword

The last published volume of my diary – *Everything to Lose* – ended with the death from a heart attack of my husband Ralph Partridge on December 1st 1960, and its final words were: 'Now I am absolutely alone and for ever.' Though I had lived under the ever-present shadow of this possibility for the previous four years, I had been sustained by bouts of irrational hope, and the blow was a crushingly final one – something in a completely different dimension from any anguish I had ever had to face before. Suicide has never seemed to me a wicked action but I am certain it is an extremely selfish one, causing pain and bitterness to those who are trying to prevent it. I was very much aware of this; also I think my life-instinct was naturally strong, and it emerged in a desire to try to 'hang on', and even to tell my closest friends that I meant to do so. What follows is the story of that struggle. But when suddenly bereft of the person I loved best, the companion with whom I had for more than thirty years kept up a river of communication which I believe was unusually wide and deep, how could I possibly choke that impulse into silence? Looking back, I feel that I only survived because I kept an outlet for my emotions, memories and speculations, instead of stifling them at birth. Why publish something so unbearably sad? I may be asked. Because virtually all adults learn sooner or later that there is a great deal of sorrow in life, that it is interrupted by disasters and crushed by stresses; that death and bereavement come to everyone and have to be faced. But most also know that it is not *all* sad, that in its very essence lies something glorious and splendid, that the stuff it is made of arouses constant wonder and interest, that even when one cannot stop crying one must suddenly laugh. So that though this volume may be full of tragedy it has a happy ending, in that it describes a sort of victory and return of courage.

I make no apology for my atheism. It is a position I reached at a very early age, and I consider it is better founded and less destructive than most religious faiths; but I do hold to my ethical values very strongly.

Ralph died at Ham Spray House. I began to write this diary a few weeks later in a small hotel on the French Riviera, where I had come with my great friends Julia (née Strachey) and Lawrence Gowing, who very kindly suggested my going with them on a visit to La Soueo, Roquebrune to value Simon Bussy's[1] paintings. I should add perhaps that none of my diaries was written for publication, nor was the first published until thirty-eight years after I had written it.

---

[1] Lytton Strachey's brother-in-law. His death and his wife's – intestate – had left problems by French law.

1960

—◦❧❦◦—

December 17th, Saturday: Hotel Mas des Héliotropes, Roquebrune, Alpes Maritimes, France

I cannot write about these last seventeen days – not *now*, anyway. Nor can I see that I shall ever want to remember them. It's been all I could do to live them. What has surprised me is that just because the blow has been so mortal, as if roughly, savagely cutting me in half and leaving me with one leg and one arm only, I am with what seems to me total illogicality under this menace struggling frantically to survive. Kitty West[1] wrote to me that Ralph had once said that if I died 'he would not go on' and I know that's true. How much more rational and logical that seems. What earthly sense in this pitiful frantic struggle? The life-instinct must be much stronger than I knew.

My instant awareness of loss was total, final and complete. He was gone, and nothing that remained had any significance for me. Yet I feel it's impossible that I can be really aware of what lies ahead and still want to live. Ergo, I'm *not* really aware of it; I have buried and suffocated some part of it, and one day I shall wake and find I've been falsely bearing the unbearable, and either kill myself or go mad.

Another discovery I have made: compared to the torture of being on the rack, the deadly fear of losing everything – *having* lost it, utter desolation is a state of calm. I have nothing to lose, I care about nothing. I may be stumbling on, blindly pushed by some extraordinary incomprehensible instinct, but I *don't care* at all. *There's nothing now that matters.*

It would be ungrateful, though, not to mention the fabulous

---

[1] First wife of Anthony West.

kindness of friends, which alters my whole view of human nature – the Carringtons,[1] the Gowings,[2] Burgo,[3] Robert,[4] each and all coming forward radiating strong beams of kindness, thoughtfulness and imaginative support.

Yet I'm painfully aware that I am a street accident exuding blood on the pavement, and it's a ghastly strain for each of them personally to be with me. They do want to help (and God knows they do) but if they could know my wounds were tied up and the flow of blood stopped, they would naturally be happier away from me. Yet with the greatest gratitude I have to accept their heroic kindness. And oh, *Janetta!*[5] – what a debt I now have to her; flying back from Greece, taking me in and making a real refuge for me at Montpelier Square with all her rare and exquisite sensitiveness, gentleness and strength. But I said I'd write no more and I won't. I'll draw another line and begin with the start of our journey yesterday. All the same, I do think the impulse to write here is perhaps salutary, a first attempt to let up the terrifying, iron clamp which I have fastened on my thoughts.

The Gowings and I left England by the Blue Train yesterday morning *en route* for the South of France. Janetta drove me to the station. I could hardly bear to leave her and felt my eyes filling with helpless tears. Like a child going to school, however, I felt better once we had started.

Julia in a deep black extinguisher of a straw hat hissed in my ear as we got into the Golden Arrow: 'I *must* fight against my terrible desire to be taken for a millionaire duchess. Too shaming!' As a traveller she is surprisingly dominant and speaks confident French.

First impact with the cruel Frogs was appalling. *No* porters rushed on board at Calais and we only by the skin of our teeth, and after countless misdirections yelled in cross voices, found our *wagons-lit* at last. After which came a sort of oblivion, followed by the usual speechless drained exhaustion about nine in the evening, not improved by the infernal racket of the dining-car. I saw

[1] Noel and Catharine.
[2] Lawrence and Julia.
[3] My son now twenty-five.
[4] Kee.
[5] Jackson. Now Parladé.

that this worried poor Julia, who tried to get me to talk about flower-collecting. Lawrence is anxious for her to stop being anxious, and the thing she's most likely to be anxious about during these three weeks is me. I'm already beginning to feel anxious about making her anxious. There's also, of course, the permanent undercurrent of her anxiety for Lawrence.

This morning, December 17th, I woke from drugged sleep to hear rain lashing the carriage window; looked out and saw water bucketing from the pale sky onto the vines which stood as it were in rivers. So it has gone on all day. When I walked up the hill to the village, I noticed the weather with detachment, but the smells, crannied plants and lights beginning to twinkle in Monte Carlo over the grey and purple sea brought a kind of balm.

December 18th

Writing letters sitting up in bed before my breakfast tray arrived, an agonizing process, drawing tears and blood. I can only do a few at a time.

December 19th

A hard day's work at La Souco in Simon Bussy's dank mould-smelling studio.[1] Lawrence seems to enjoy his role as general, ordering Julia and me kindly about. While he dictated the names and measurements of Simon's pictures I wrote them down, and Julia labelled and stacked them, Lawrence striding about like a large bird with a stalking movement that seemed to be going to lay him flat on his nose any moment, and making a running commentary on the little pictures clutched in his large clumsy-seeming hands.

'A *marvellous* painter, what a marvellous painter! . . . This is simply terrible . . . Simon's sense of humour! There's something

---

[1] When Dorothy Bussy, sister of Lytton Strachey, died intestate the lawyers discovered that eleven *héritiers* must share her estate in differing proportions dictated by French law. Lawrence Gowing had been commissioned to come out to Roquebrune and value her husband Simon Bussy's pictures in his studio here. Simon Bussy was a contemporary and friend of Matisse; his paintings were largely of birds and fish, but include fine portraits of his family and French writers.

grizzly about it . . . Ah, I see what it is, every bird or fish is a self-portrait.'

There's no better anodyne than work, and it hammered me for a while into a sort of unconsciousness. Walk through the fantastically picturesque village with Julia. Mild soft light on the silvery sea; roses, mimosa and geranium in flower but no sun. When ten o'clock came round I toppled into bed and despairing desolation. Can I possibly go on? The word NEVER echoed horribly through my brain and I lay flat and passive under the repetitive pain of it. But I said I wouldn't write of it and what is the use? I'll only *en passant* note that the life-instinct makes it impossible for me to think either backwards or forwards, and I live uneasily on a tiny island of the dreadful present.

December 20th

Interesting session with the La Souco books morning and afternoon; I've discovered some things of possible value. Then I plunged down the cliff to the Lower Corniche in an attempt to meet Burgo's bus from Nice. After a long wait and a talk with a friendly flat-chested spinster from the 'village', I gave up and toiled up the steps in the darkness. Burgo came later in a taxi from the airport. I think it was salutary for me to have to brisk up on his behalf.

December 21st

Sun all day. Burgo and I lunched out of doors after a morning's work at La Souco, and afterwards walked to Menton. It's a large town and I shrivelled with fear and loneliness when I thought of my plan to move there later, into the great charmless barrack of the Hotel des Ambassadeurs among buses and shops where Clive and Barbara[1] have elected to stay. It's time to describe this place. Roquebrune village is all steps, *petits coins* stuffed with cats, winding tunnels. A castle stands at the top of a steep hill and this hotel on a promontory near the precipitous bottom, with a terraced garden of roses, geraniums and cacti. This other-worldly eyrie, staring out over the sea to Monte Carlo, proves the refuge I need,

---

[1] Clive Bell and Barbara Bagenal had thrown in their lots together, and were inseparable until Clive died in 1964.

as well as anything could, by its gothic unreality. I took an immediate fancy to my room. It faces sea and sun, is furnished in simple Provençal style with red curtains and covers and the floor painted with red which comes off on my bare feet. I can make a little nest here in which to return and lick my wounds, but my heart fails me at the thought of doing so in Menton. There are sunny corners to sit in and stare at the sea between palms and cacti. There are twelve cats whose emotional life I can brood over stupidly by the hour. The dining-room is the only indoors public room, lined artily with logs with the bark on and straw-covered lamps. The food is simply *first-rate*. Monsieur Pons, the patron, is a short, *more* than spherical man – i.e. wider than high, with a short beard and kind brown eyes, a painter. Slightly lame, he rolls along on his short fat legs, till I'm afraid of seeing him bowl off down the steep hill. His wife, a skilled cook, is an intellectual. She speaks excellent English and German. She is rather hunched, ill-looking, dressed curiously in trousers and a sort of medieval hood, has a beautiful nervous, worn face and a low melodious voice. There are various grandparents in the offing, and two small children.

December 22nd

I notice no-one ever mentions Ralph's name to me, though I often do to them. I find this horribly unearthly. Julia and Lawrence are endlessly kind to me, and I do hope Julia's worry for me is not exhausting her. This morning she came into my room to say she would stay on till Clive and Barbara arrived, letting Lawrence go home alone. I tried to protest, but she waved my protests away and tears welled up to contradict my words.

Letters 'of sympathy' still arrive and I toil painfully through the answers. I long to hear from friends like Janetta, Joan Cochemé, Robert or Mary;[1] but naturally no-one wants to think about me, though they wish me well. Only my own efforts can make me otherwise than a black spot to be avoided, and I have no strength to make efforts.

---

[1] Campbell (now Dunn).

December 28th

So the days pass. A sort of routine takes shape and I'm getting better at dealing with the surface of things. Rather to my surprise I find I want to be alone quite a lot in my room. When my thoughts grow unbearable I either translate[1] (in the day-time) or take to dope at night.

I bitterly regret that last night I upset Julia by talking cynically about vitamins! They belong to her scientific credo, and I resolve never to do such a thing again. Relations with Burgo are curiously normal, as if the parental element had been wiped out; but I think he's restless at not hearing from either Simon Raven or Anthony Blond.[2]

December 29th

Julia has heroically swallowed any rancour she may have felt, and is as kind and good to me as ever. Bad day, however. My thread of life is very thin. Julia and I to Monte Carlo in the afternoon. Though fascinated by the worldly materialistic Edwardian architecture – every motif in key – I was also depressed by its soulless flavour of greed. Burgo gloomy, or irritated by Julia, in the evening. Off to my solitary room, and little sleep, staring into a world which seems gimcrack and papery, and not improved by the French letting off another atom bomb in the Sahara.

December 30th

Two days of radiant sun, and sky a deep rich blue. Ups and downs – why write of them? The beauty of the sea when it turns pale tin-colour at night, of the translucent sky in the morning, fronds, flowers and so forth, is like something seen through a glass screen a long way off and out of reach. They don't *really* touch me though I can catalogue their virtues. Cataloguing is about all I'm good for.

With Burgo to Menton yesterday, a long walk, right to the old port. Certainly a day that is filled is a better day and because I've sagged today I feel the worse for it.

[1] I had the job of translating a book on alcoholism from the French.
[2] Two of Burgo's friends, writer and publisher.

Monsieur Pons came in to dinner wearing a ferocious grimace. He told us he had an appalling '*rage des dents*'. This morning he was doped and rather excitable, flinging his stout little limbs about and embarrassing Lawrence with his talk about art. I'm sad I get no letter from Janetta, but posts are appallingly slow.

December 31st

I see it is vital to keep a tight grip on my reins; any loosening of them, any momentary wondering what to do next, is fatal. I simply *must* make the decision, however arbitrary, to do *something* – it hardly matters what. At moments I feel I am best alone. At others a dreadful panic of this endless colloquy with myself arises in me, making my heart gallop.

Natural history of the Gowings: so long as Lawrence can arrange his day to allow of writing, painting and plenty of sleep he is the happiest man alive. He has no desire whatever for expeditions, discoveries, change or social stimulation.

Julia is of course in a perpetual state of dissatisfaction with her environment, for all the intense pleasure she may get in watching cats, or in the ambience of this place. Yet even in that she's very capricious. This has always been a key place to her ever since her childhood's visits to the Bussys at La Souco or her writing *Cheerful Weather*[1] here; she thinks of it as the one place where life was run on oiled wheels and she could sail ahead without obstacles into her 'creative writing', as she always calls it. The first few days here she was day-dreaming with Lawrence about buying or renting a villa here. 'Julia has "twigs in her beak" ', he said. We even went and looked at one – she and I – a couple of tiny cell-like rooms with no amenities. Soon afterwards she announced that she had no desire whatever to live here.

Last night I was talking to Lawrence about the obstacles one felt to setting to work. How I justified not sitting down to translate by saying, 'In this mood I know I'll do it badly'. He thought one *should* sit down and try, because by overcoming the obstacle, one sometimes did one's best work. (This in fact I had done earlier in

[1] Her first book, *Cheerful Weather for the Wedding*, published by Chatto & Windus in 1932.

the evening, but without this happy result.) Julia resented this because it didn't consort with her view that the 'creative writer' – but none of us except her is that – must wait until 'the spirit calls', or 'the unconscious takes over'. I forget exactly how she worded it. In fact it was hardly ever possible for him or her to operate. I'm struck by the amount she *excludes* from life – the whole political world (so does Lawrence almost as much, neither of them wants to read the paper), a large part of literature, all music.

1961

January 2nd

Dick and Simonette[1] came over from Nice to lunch on Saturday. Julia, Burgo and I went down to La Souco to meet them on their way up from the bus. When they appeared outside the French windows I almost laughed aloud. Dick looked as if he'd come to a funeral, in a deep black, long undertaker's overcoat and black hat, moving at a snail's pace, his eyes bulging in his white apprehensive face. Simonette's looks are still very fine. She wore a black 'busby' pulled over her eyes, tight London suit, black stockings and pin-heels. (Julia afterwards defended her 'heroism' in tackling the cobbled steps in these heels. 'But for what?' I asked. 'Aesthetic effect,' said Julia.) Simonette certainly came full of suspicion on behalf of the Bussy *héritiers*, of whom Dick is one, and made several remarks like 'It's all quite different', 'Where's everything *gone?*', 'But where have things been tidied *to?*' and so on. They say John[2] is doing his level best to bugger everything up, has consulted agents and solicitors on his own and is convinced that Pippa, Marjorie[3] and probably everyone else want to deprive him of his rights. By the end of lunch we had, I think, convinced Dick and Simonette that if John went on in that way no-one would get a penny. But Dick's line is that he is a Quietist – translated into common English he's so lazy that he won't do a thing, even in his own interests.

I felt quite ashamed of our funereal guests when I led them

---

[1] Richard Strachey, nephew of Lytton, and his wife.
[2] Dick's younger brother, another *héritier*.
[3] Lytton's unmarried sisters.

onto the hotel terrace and they ungraciously made no greeting or acknowledgement to Monsieur Pons.

This is all pretty dull, but it has been the only intrusion from the outside world, so it was a relief to have to think of it. The first day of 1961 was dripping and foggy, cold, dank and pitch dark. Feeling as I do, on the rack all the time, these outward misfortunes make no difference. I'm in a Japanese concentration camp anyway and expect nothing more than survival. But for what? Heaven knows.

A lot of letters on Saturday including one from Janetta, lovely and long.

January 3rd

I'm worried about Julia and her arrangement to stay on with me here. She doesn't write her book, and never will. Yesterday there was a great parade of shutting herself in her room with it – but she dozed and read a detective story all afternoon. Contacts and general conversation are reduced to meal-times and seldom get anywhere. My heart bleeds for Burgo, who is doing very well in suppressing his youthful impatience, to make it fit in with Julia's strict boarding-house rules. One of these is that after our dinner is finished we sit in creaking chairs round a basket table and *no-one speaks*, for fear of distracting anyone who is reading. I find this strangely inhuman. Last night Burgo was in a lively mood, wanting to talk about *The Journal to Stella* which he was reading, and being quite interesting about it. Pinched disapproval from Julia, whose eyes were bent unseeingly on the *New Statesman*. She and I have not made much contact lately. I would have liked to discuss the problems that face me in the future – but feel she doesn't want to; and she has still never *once* mentioned Ralph's name. What a relief it was to get a long, moving, excellent letter from Gerald[1] yesterday, almost all about him. Yet Julia is heroic in her intentions and it's ungrateful to find fault with the result, especially as I feel her anxiety for me is spoiling what ought to have been a holiday for her. I would really rather she returned to England with Lawrence than leave me feeling responsible for her unease.

[1] Brenan.

I somehow do manage to work and I clutch at it like a drowning man. I have to – I'd sink otherwise, not that I do it effectively or well.

The nicest thing yesterday was a walk up the hill with Burgo in the afternoon, finding some wild flowers. And in the morning a pile of letters – Mary, Raymond,[1] Joan again, Gerald, Gamel,[2] Heywood.[3] Alas, there's no-one left to write to me.

January 5th

When Julia came into my room I tried to say that I didn't want her to make sacrifices for me, that – much as I should enjoy her company – I would be quite all right alone, but I have only to speak of such things and the silly helpless tears well up and brim over. She was kind, sweet and good, and while I was in the bath left a little note in my room which touched me deeply, begging me to say no more about it. 'When something happens to you it *literally* happens to all your friends.'

Burgo is my chief anxiety now. Anthony Blond doesn't send him his *laisser-passer* to Monte Carlo, nor does Simon communicate his plans.[4] The poor boy is therefore literally in the air and getting increasingly, and I think justifiably, angry with Simon. What of that apparently benign and genial, but arrestedly juvenile figure? Burgo also told me that when they met last in London and he wanted to talk to Simon about his childhood feelings about Ralph, Simon merely said: 'You never liked him, did you?' which was very obtuse.

It looks anyway as if Julia and I have another week here. I think of it as 'doing time' and try to avoid remembering that nothing lies beyond but more time. What Burgo will do if he still hears nothing from Simon (to whom he wired yesterday) I don't know. Lawrence leaves us the day after tomorrow.

Yesterday John Strachey and Peggy Bainbridge[5] came to La Souco and back here to tea. John seems about to see reason,

---

[1] Mortimer.
[2] Brenan.
[3] Hill.
[4] To meet Burgo abroad.
[5] Later his wife.

however, about the Bussy inheritance, and is going to sign up all right, on condition that a lawyer he favours will be given the job of dealing with things. Lawrence at once agreed, so all was hunky-dory.

January 7th

An odd afternoon in Monte Carlo yesterday, all four of us going to the extraordinary and beautiful aquarium. Strange that fish should have expressions so vividly suggesting human moods: *deep* disapproval, despair, evil hatred, coquetry. One of the must curious species had a broad bulging head like an owl, great blue eyes with fluttering lids, a little rosebud mouth, and was constantly on the move with quick scatty movements and golden flapping fins. It looked like a chorus-girl crossed with an owl.

January 8th

Yesterday morning brought a letter from Simon for Burgo and at least some definite news to relieve the waiting-room atmosphere. He 'can't possibly get to Tunis before February 17th, if then,' – no reason given – 'but will be going off skiing in Austria for a fortnight' instead of meeting Burgo in Tunis. He describes his own behaviour as 'treacherous' and says he will 'crawl' to Burgo when he sees him. Burgo seems relieved at least to have certainty where there was chaos and confusion. There were tranquil episodes today (a lovely day). In the afternoon Burgo and I had an adventurous walk ending in a wilderness of brambles and huge stones covered in herbage, and my all but losing my trowel and my botany spectacles, thrown out of my basket by the impact. Burgo was patient and angelic, spending twenty minutes looking for them with me, and at last we found them. In the evening we lost dear Lawrence – a great sadness to see him go off in the darkness.

January 9th, afternoon

Burgo's troubles seem endless. Today he heard from Poppet[1] that her step-daughter is already in 'his' flat, so he has nowhere to go

---

[1] Pol, Augustus John's daughter, whose flat Burgo had rented.

if he does go back to London. This excruciating business of trying to share his burdens is finishing what sanity I had left, and I cannot be in his presence and not share them. Today great wafts of loneliness have found cracks and crevices and come washing in. Tears, blood and sweat.

An intense smell of cats fills the hotel today; the little boy croaks and coughs. It has been gloriously fine, however, and we walked to Gorbio, lunched there and came home by bus.

January 12th

It's almost a surprise to find myself still alive, still here. Burgo has done very well, pulling himself together with an effort, and has booked himself a flight back to England on Sunday.

This evening he and I move to join Clive at Menton (Burgo for three nights only) and Julia returns to England. My tremulous fear of change is under hatches. I'm braced, and almost longing to get out of the dense smell of cats and the coughs here. A full stop of a sort, some fixed plans, and on I go, *somehow* or other.

Yesterday we travelled by train in pelting rain to lunch with John Strachey[1] and his Peggy. John is reviving his persecution mania about the Bussy inheritance. A nice man called Basil Leng was there, and took us to the Picasso and Léger exhibitions, afterwards driving us all the way back to Roquebrune – no longer home.

January 17th: Hotel des Ambassadeurs, Menton

I've been quite ill the last three days, with enough of a fever to make me consent to see the doctor who came to see the *patron's* wife on Sunday – a little dynamic Groucho Marx, who rushed in, shot questions at me, sounded me, took my blood-pressure and prescribed antibiotics and stuff to rub into my back. As my temperature rose, and as during the night I choked and sweated, I wondered of course how ill I was going to be and thought hopefully of death! Here was a threat to my precarious life-instinct . . . What

---

[1] John acted with sudden brilliance a few months later. He got expert advice as to the value of the Bussy pictures, bought out all the other *héritiers* and put the pictures up for sale, so making a handsome sum!

did I feel? I asked myself in one of the endless colloquies that take the place of my conversations with Ralph. That I longed to be dead but couldn't bear the thought of dying (pictured as lying in a French hospital with tubes up my nose, squalid, lonely and frightened). I suppose millions of people feel both these things, and the ones who act logically and take overdoses are just braver, or madder – or what? In some strange way, the worst thing that has ever happened to me in my life has made me feel saner than before.

Barbara and Clive were in this hotel on Thursday night and until I went to bed on Saturday afternoon I thought both of them were going to drive me mad – Clive by his frantic fussing about everything (particularly being late – he dashes in to meals at 12.30 and 7.00 if he can) and Barbara by her repetitive chatter. But since I've been in bed she has been so kind and helpful that I feel quite conscience-stricken to think what I wrote to Janetta about her. Burgo left on Sunday; since coming here he was as sweet, kind and thoughtful as possible and I shed tears to see him go. None the less, I hope he will soon make himself a life apart from me, chiefly for his sake.

This illness (I'm nearly well, thanks to dynamic Groucho) has put my power to stand solitude to the test, and it's not come out too badly. I can not only fill long hours with reading and writing but think to myself for quite long periods, although it's thinking of a wretchedly poor quality, dismally needing the stimulus that Ralph's more creative mind gave it. There is a vast area that I still can't force my mind to enter – or only by making little tentative dashes. Though in theory I know that everything ought to be explored and faced, the instinct of self-preservation prevents me. There's also the fact that it's as if a piece – half – of me had gone. What is left is not exactly bereaved, it's *incomplete*.

January 18th

Better. I'm somehow fortified by having got through this ordeal by isolation, although there was a moment of panic yesterday when I thought I shouldn't. Groucho visited me last night and has allowed me up in my room today and tomorrow, and down on Friday. In his magnetic mesmeric way he convinced me I must do as he said. Raymond[1] arrived last night, sent up a huge gorgeous bunch of carnations from Nice market which glorify my room, telephoned me, and came to see me this morning. He has been a great tonic to me, setting going some degree of that communicable fluid which does not flow in chats with Little Barbara. I am rather saddened by Clive, who seems to have stepped quite a long way out of this world into the next, but perhaps there's still some recuperative bounce in him.

It has been something to be allowed to bath and dress and eat my disgusting lunch at my table, and also a good post has come, letters from Heywood, Julia and Janetta.

January 19th

A visit from Raymond last night cheered me to the extent of leaving me quite over-excited. Off his own bat he mentioned Clive's having suddenly become an old man, so fussy and nervous, and also Barbara's chatter being so exasperating: 'Do you think you and I will be as nervous as that if we live to be eighty?' he asked. No, I don't, or anyway not so timid, so craven, for that is what is the matter with Clive as with Dick Strachey who cannot go by aeroplane and will never go to a cinema or live in an upper floor for fear of fire.

January 20th

Left my prison and found it was still with me. The whole world is a prison to me and I seem to have adopted the humble, crushed attitude of a person in a concentration camp, expecting nothing – certainly not happiness – glad to have the attention of a prison mouse or spider, futilely grateful to be alive.

Outside it is cold, or Groucho would have let me out. Instead I spent an hour or so in the glassed-in verandah watching some sour-faced French matrons chattering together (mice and spiders) and lunched alone with Clive, while Raymond and Barbara went to Ventimiglia.

Natural history of Clive and Barbara: yesterday I went to sit in

---

[1] Mortimer. His visit was an act of self-effacing kindness. He had a morbid fear of germs.

Barbara's room in the morning. Discussing her false teeth for some reason, she took them out and laid them close beside me on the table! I could hardly believe my eyes. In the evening Clive visited me and I had to try not to laugh at his long preoccupied tussle with the zip of his flies which wouldn't stay done up.

January 22nd

The breakfast waiter has a very strange way of intoning, singing almost, as he comes in with my tray: 'Bon *JOUR*!!! Ca*FÉ*!! La *NEIGE*!! La *PLUIE*!!' he intones pessimistically. I do in fact look out and see a sky of dirty grey cotton-wool fitting down close over my mountain's round forehead. Yesterday I went out, however, to lunch with Raymond in a fish restaurant in the port and felt much the better for it, until Groucho (who had come to look at Clive's leg, swollen after slipping on some steps) depressed me unutterably by saying accusingly: 'You are *not well* yet. You are *cheerful* because your temperature is down, but you still have a spot on your lung and it might all begin again.' Result: hardly any sleep last night and cough worse today. I couldn't help fancying it was with delight that he found from the X-ray that poor Clive has cracked his tibia. It's all for the worst in the worst of all possible worlds. Clive sat dejected like a small boy disappointed of a treat and said that if he was confined to his room he would throw himself out of the window. Raymond strode round the room arguing with Groucho. Clive has to be put in plaster today, and will stay up for a day or so, so the sickroom atmosphere continues. Poor Raymond!

After dinner there was an extraordinary scene from an eighteenth-century comedy in Clive's bedroom. He lay in bed without his teeth while Raymond and I sat round arguing about the relation between love and money.

I put the question about my future to Raymond. He is *not* in favour of my living in London, says he finds it every year less sympathetic. I must try and tabulate my friends' views . . . Meanwhile my concentration-camp life is likely to go on and I need some more mice and spiders.

Raymond is very stimulating, almost too much so for my weakened wits. They respond in a way to his electric charge and then go whirring futilely all night long.

January 23rd

Bad to worse. Barbara and Raymond took Clive to the clinique where his leg was put in plaster but the surgeon told Barbara he was not to use it for *five weeks*. She seemed on the brink of tears and collapse (I can't blame her) and said Clive must not be told. Oh, the sadness of old age! If two days in his room made him want to *se jeter par la fenêtre*, what now?

Terrific undertakings, moving all Clive and Barbara's things to a suite with a bathroom at the end of the passage. Raymond and I scurried to and fro carrying Clive's pathetic possessions. Staff, usually so friendly, in a rage at this. Ambulance men carrying Clive upstairs, who even in this predicament was able to catch sight of himself in a looking-glass and pat at his wig. The tragi-comic effect of this masquerade of clowns! I do *not* include Raymond, who has remained dignified, elegant and sweet-tempered throughout. After Clive had been installed in bed, Raymond, Barbara and I drove off up the Gorbio valley to a smart, expensive restaurant got up in peasant style, with gigots of lamb revolving and blackening on a spit over a roaring fire and a terrible tenor caterwauling to a guitar. This meal was rather a nightmare to me as my voice vanished completely. By evening, Clive was in tears, Barbara also, and Raymond beginning to panic on his own account. Slept well but am still voiceless, damn it.

January 24th

Yesterday was pretty desperate. By evening suicide thoughts were in the ascendant. Also other thoughts of flying back to England at once. *What am I doing here?* Heaven knows. Appeals to me from Barbara to help keep Clive's spirits up; and I gladly would, but how can I with not an ounce of spirits of my own and no shred of voice to simulate them with? This last hampers me dreadfully – I can do some sort of perfunctory flapping with words, but without them I sink into patent glumness. What use going out with Raymond to a noisy restaurant when I can't utter? I said I would stay in, therefore, in the glassed-in verandah and try and get rid of the great toad which sits on my chest and paralyses my vocal chords and – I must admit – fills me with terror of being sent back to solitary confinement. All day I was hiding from Groucho, scared stiff of his accusing 'You are NOT well yet.'

January 27th

Yesterday Raymond left, angelic to the last. I had had a severe panic the night before, lying awake dreading the close quarters, the married life as it were that lay ahead with Clive and Barbara in their flat at Garavan, as they have kindly asked me. This flat, large and spacious with a nice garden, has two big and lovely bedrooms but really no place for a third person – except a slit containing a bed like a *wagon-lit* bunk, with no wardrobe, nothing. Barbara has a nannie's desire to involve us all in each other's physical functioning, and this I most emphatically don't share. Just as to Nannie the sight of a baby sitting on his pot is sweet and funny and the be-all and end-all of her life, she would like all the barriers and reticences to go down between adults. So I now diagnose her setting her false teeth beside me on the table as a symbol of the same attitude that makes her trot to bring Clive his yellow box of false teeth ('Buttercup'), when he wants to eat. (Campaigning by Raymond and me made him put them in more often, but now Raymond's gone he's given that up and is toothless all day.) And yesterday *pour comble*, Barbara wanted me to stay in the room while Clive *fit pipi* as they will both call it. That settled it. A glorious day yesterday – and I walked off by myself around the bay of Garavan to try and find somewhere where I could live *en demi-pension* and lunch in their flat each day. The grand Hotel des Anglais offered me a small room at the back. I was rather nervous how Barbara would take this, as she had begged for 'support' with a little clutching claw on my arm the night before. And she took it very well. I was able to put it as a form of consideration for them. Immense relief.

Financial ruin, but what does that matter!

Barbara and I and Miss Newlands, a tall thin old Highland lady with wide bird's eyes and a little white owlet's fluff drifting from her head, went to a concert of chamber music last night.

26

January 28th

My bid for independence has set me up quite a little. I must now contrive to *take* that independence.

The microcosm of the hotel inhabitants – increasing in number daily – points almost every grim moral in the calendar. Loneliness, boredom, boasting, desire to be thought well of by their fellows, stare out at one from every side. And having to suffer in public as it were, makes them cosset themselves in drawling tones of unreal casualness. Everyone is becoming unbearably friendly. Even Miss Newlands overdid it a bit yesterday, coming and standing over our table as we ate.

Miss Daniels, a deep-voiced lady who thinks herself dashing and talks of 'Monte', came and puffed lozenges in my face, to tell me she was so interested in Raymond having written about Younghusband as he was a relation of hers.

'Of course Helen Younghusband was a maniac,' I understood her to say.

'Dear me, how dreadful!' I was on the point of answering, but realized in time she meant 'Magniac'.

One gets people very wrong at times. An elderly lady smiling incessantly, whom Raymond placed as paid companion to another she was with, turns out to be Lady Crawfurd, and approached me beaming to ask if I too was a Crawfurd, as I was wearing their tartan. Horrors! I now rather like her, but as with Miss Newlands, the Highland accent gives a foreign charm.

Elderly grey-haired lady who must fifty years ago have been handsome: 'They say Queen – Eleanor, was it? – had Calais written on her heart. Well, I've got SUEZ written on mine. I shall never forget it, never.'

Stout red-faced party (male) with bronchitis to the above lady: 'Oh, yes, I always get out of England each winter. I went to Majorca one year, and to Cannes another. That's where I had my *affair.*'

Lady (dreadfully embarrassed) – 'Oh, that sounds very exciting!' (Changing the subject) 'Did you like Cannes?'

Stout party: 'Yes, but you see, one gets so lonely. Then I met this *dear* Lady Portman, who was eighty-six. Very intelligent, charming woman. When I left I gave her a huge bunch of flowers and she looked up at me with half-closed eyes and said, 'Naughty!' Well, *I* call that an affair.'

January 29th

A fine day, and I got through it steadily without panics or collapse. I, Clive – sat while Barbara lunched out again, and again he became adult the moment she left, saying, 'Be a good boy'. I suppose she can't help it, and today irritation was supplanted by wonder – and also almost admiration for a certain courage she has as well as good humour. Yesterday Clive's only lapse was to say whiningly, 'Where's my lacky?' 'Your WHAT?' 'My lacky – oh, you'll never find it.' This turned out to be an elastic band he puts round his spectacle case. Then there's his 'tinkly winkly medicine'!

January 31st

The last two days I've taken long walks by myself up the hills, clutching at the rope-ladder of my visual impressions, rejecting with some success the pointless imaginary conversations liable to invade my head. The two cemeteries on their twin hills were the objects of my first walk. A madwoman in a fur stole, talking aloud and waving her arms like King Lear. Italian-looking children speaking French. A solid little girl carrying a black cat uphill in loving embracing arms. At the upper cemetery a widow in deep black dabbing her eyes with a handkerchief and confiding in her taxi-driver.

Last night the doctor rushed in to see Clive and he is to come down in his chair to lunch today but mustn't walk for a fortnight. Little Barbara has just been in for sympathy this morning – Clive is fussing because she has a hairdresser's appointment (an inch of grey hair has appeared each side of her parting). Will I dress him? Oh, God, is there no way of avoiding her dragging me in as second nurse? I've suggested she change her appointment to this afternoon, and she says she'll try.

She did, and a good job too, seeing the frenzy of nerves Clive got into over being dressed, even by Barbara. What would it have been like if I had tried? We've had 'potty' and 'eidy' today; what next?

It's been a marvellous day, warm, soft, still and fine, the mountains' edge sharp against the blue sky but a few hanging wreaths of cloud. Again I've walked myself to a standstill, this time to Cap Martin, but come back almost in tears. Along the front one meets so many couples of all ages affectionately walking arm-in-arm with their mates, and I feel nothing but *brute envy* of them. Rather panicked about being unable to steer my thoughts, until by dint of walking I stupefied myself into one big eye. There are always strange sights to see. On Cap Martin sat a white-haired lady listening to Bach on a very good portable wireless, and what seemed to be a poet was staring at the waves coming in over the shingle and adding a line from moment to moment.

Perhaps these solitary walks are going to be too much. Between the Scylla of solitude and the Charybdis of Barbara's conversation I don't know what to do . . .

February 1st

These pitiful scribblings are like scratches on the vast monolith of my desolation, and I only go on having recourse to them because they are in some way an outlet. Alas, I can't tell Ralph what a desert my life is without him, describe the extraordinary wooden unreality of it. Nor can I tell Barbara and Clive. They are Arthur Prince dummies to practise the sound of my voice with. Yet I *can't* get down to the deeper areas of my misery – because it's a region so painful that the scalpel (being held in my own hand) recoils instinctively from the exposed nerve.

We got Clive downstairs to lunch and dinner in his wheel-chair in the lift. It cheered him up enormously and he sat up till his usual bed-time, 9.15.

February 4th

I moved to the Hotel des Anglais yesterday afternoon. Though my bedroom is smaller and scruffier, the plaster crumbles, the handle of the wardrobe comes off at a touch, the basin refuses to hold water – the rest of the hotel is grander than the Ambassadeurs. The dining-room is immense and stately with parquet floor (over which many waiters shoot about like comets, pushing vast sluggards' delights); there are several enormous lounges and a useful 'writing-room'. In this I sat down stubbornly to work at about four, and from then till now I've not seen a soul to speak to. It seems to me instead of a recuperative treatment, I'm subjecting myself to some hideous test or punishment here. Can't think what I'm at. Again the desire to fly home has appeared. Why, why, why have I returned to the life of a scribbling schoolgirl in this solitude? Yet there is the blue sky stretched above the mimosa-clad hill.

February 5th

An awful night, but morning is always better, and the pure intense blue sky still stretches up over the hill. During the night I felt it was madness to stay on here, subjecting myself to this unutterable isolation – I longed to be back at Ham Spray with Dinah.[1] But the trouble is I don't want to be *anywhere* – I want to be away from wherever I am. When I'm in this grizzly hotel I want to be with Clive and Barbara. When I'm with them I want to get away as fast as possible. I want to be nowhere. I want desperately to be dead, but can't face, or can't think how to achieve that happy state.

So this morning I'm undecided, and have no-one to thrash out my problems with. I must in any case stay here a week or so, because of letters. Then I will try to alter my technique. New plan for living – work late, to get over the *ghastly* evenings? More blue pills. More sun and exercise.

February 6th

I really rather 'enjoyed myself' yesterday afternoon, perversely enough, walking into Italy along the Blackpool-like main road, and back home under the great prehistoric cliff and the Grotte des Enfants.

Today I went to drink cocktails with Maybud Campbell[2] at her glorious villa. Basil Leng there, with two queers from the Ambassadeurs.

Clive is low and depressed again, leaves out his teeth and says he wishes he was dead. Rosetta, the Italian maid, kept repeating, '*Povera Rosetta, molte tribulazioni*' as she served lunch: Barbara went on and on about her collar-bone, broken many years ago. Her power to irritate me seems to have been raised to burning-

---

[1] My black cat.
[2] Professional botanist, to whom I had an introduction.

point by proximity under difficult circumstances. And I too have my *tribulazioni*, which I sometimes think they forget. I've got through today without sinking too far into the pit and with only a few tears. I'll say no more. This hotel is really maddening – it deliberately sets itself to produce *cuisine Anglaise* – roast meat and boiled potatoes *every single day*!

February 7th, 7.30

Sitting up in bed, trying to sort out the fragments of my life and make a little sense of it. If I worked hard at my translation I could finish it in about three weeks. Should I do that and then go home? Or join Anne and Heywood[1] in Paris? Move to Clive and Barbara's flat? I'm terrified of trying yet another change only to find I can't stand it – for the real fact is I can't bear living without Ralph. But I must stop saying that. I've *got* to bear it and a lot more, too. Or get out.

February 10th

The terrible example of self-pity going on at the Clos de Peyronnet[2] has helped give a fillip to my courage. Barbara again said how desperately sorry Clive was for himself; but he has only to wait and he will be exactly as he was before he broke his leg. I think with admiration and love of Ralph's patience when he had to lie up for three weeks on far more serious terms.

So, these three last days have been more bearable, though I still hate the way I'm forced to push Ralph out of my thoughts just in order to endure each day in turn.

Marvellous weather still, and a sort of strength has invaded me just from having survived that deep, deep dip.

February 11th

Woke at five-thirty and now the black sky is navy blue. Last night I found another letter from Janetta saying she's going to ski near Briançon, along with Renée Fedden and Rosemary Hinchinbrooke,

---

[1] Hill.
[2] The villa in which Clive and Barbara had rented a flat.

and won't I join her for a week? I also thought of spending a day or two in Paris as the Hills would be there, and wrote to Derek Jackson[1] asking if I could stay a few days in his flat. He sent a wire saying, 'Very welcome'.

Anyway, Briançon or not, the future is less blank now. It has some small escape-hatches. I have noticed a desire to say NO to everything, and also to pare down my life in consonance with the Japanese Concentration Camp parallel, do without things like whiskey which I might enjoy, and force myself to an iron routine of work. It occurs to me I'm doing penance, punishing myself because I couldn't keep Ralph alive. This complicates a decision such as whether to join Janetta in the snow. I hate snow, really. Does this make me want to go as a punishment, or not go as self-indulgence?

Yesterday I lunched with a new friend – a little nippy, lively white-haired Mrs Stuart-Mackenzie who is a cousin of Pin's,[2] in a villa wonderfully placed on the road to Castellar. A great chatterer, spouting red herrings and *non sequiturs*, warm-hearted, amusing, likeable. We sat in the sun and talked very easily, but not following anything quite to its limits. I could say more to her about my real thoughts than to Little Barbara, I do believe. Or do I hurl myself meaninglessly into something new – the Yes-man uppermost for a moment?

February 16th

After my last entry I took a great haul at invisible boot-straps and somehow managed to brace up and pull myself together. The spectacle of the self-pity over at the Villa is really a moral lesson. Also, I see from my friends' letters that my extra gloom lately has been conveyed to them in mine, and they are worrying about me. This won't do; I can't just become a public nuisance. After letting the picture of being on Janetta's snowy mountain soak in my mind for a bit I fished it out and found almost nothing but fear and horror at the thought of drawing iced air into my lungs instead of this, which is balmy, carnation-laden. Of clanking funiculars and that maniac, ruthlessly competitive, obsessional winter-sports

---

[1] Ex-husband of Janetta.
[2] Clodagh, wife of Colin Mackenzie; old and dear friends living in Skye.

world. On the other side, the real delight of being with Janetta every evening and the gratification of my desire *to escape* which I know for what it is. So I've written to say no.

Well, this great effort to pull myself together worked, much to my surprise, and again produced that sense of being strengthened by the mere fact of overcoming horrors. (Robin Campbell, who has a talent for saying encouraging things, says in a letter I had yesterday, 'Your life does not sound all mimosa, but in some strange way I slightly envy the lonely and up to a point fortifying life of the hotel in winter. I'm sure it does recharge mental batteries, but then one needs something to use the accumulated power on. I have no doubt at all that you will manage this too.')

Clive has passed another stage and now puts feet to ground. He sometimes gets irritated with Barbara and says quite tartly, 'I'm never allowed to get a WORD in edgewise.' Nor is he, nor am I, and yesterday her delaying by chattering when Clive was waiting to be helped onto the sunny balcony made him angrier than I ever saw him in his life.

A letter from Bunny[1] with a weird compliment: 'You are infinitely refreshing – like the advertisement of some detergent or soap that takes the film of dirt and despair away from one'!

Well, when I come up to my lonely little bedroom I find nothing at all refreshing there (the chambermaid will shut the window at night): it seems to be full of the sour aroma of sorrow, and I recognize it as mine.

February 17th

I watched the total eclipse two mornings ago and I never expect to see a better one. It was due to be total at eight-thirty, my breakfast time. My bedroom piece of sky turned an unearthly lavender colour very gradually about eight, and tucking in my nightgown and putting on a skirt and my fur coat I went down to the hall. Looks of complicity and faint embarrassment on the faces of porters, *valets de chambre*, etc. We were all engaged on something a little queer. Outside was deathly stillness, each palm tree leaf transfixed, and the pure sky over the milky calm sea was a huge Covent Garden stage for the prima donna, the sun. One or

---

[1] David Garnett.

two watchers leaning on the balustrade the other side of the road – the dress-circle. I ordered my breakfast tray in the glassed-in porch full of potted plants, and while I ate it saw with a thrill that the obvious bite out of the sun's side was gradually increasing. The climax was astonishingly swift. Darkness rushed over the earth, yet it was never very intense. The encroaching shape seemed to make a sudden move and step right in front of the sun and then it was bang in the middle, with an unequal fringe of light all round and some glowing red carbuncles here and there on the very edge. Horrors! One carbuncle was swelling, expanding, blowing out like a great balloon. And I saw that it was the sun beginning to come out the other side – why did it look so different going in and coming out? The act was over; it seemed to have been staged for me alone. It was beautiful, strange and exciting – but no unexpected wave of emotion surged through me, no mystical thoughts about the nature of the universe, no sense of evil nor primeval fear. But I'm very, very glad to have seen it, and went up to my room in a state of catharsis. It's the first thing I can say I've enjoyed for itself.

A tune was running in my head. What was it? I suddenly realized: *Total Eclipse* from Handel's *Samson*. I took the bus after lunch to St Agnes, a village clinging to a mountain 2,000 feet up. The drive up was appalling: crowded bus, no springs, we ground up slowly in first gear, round terrifying bends where it was impossible to pass and we often had to back to get round. Up there in the fresh mountain air I looked down on the valleys wearing scarves of haze and up at the tremendous circle of mountains. Sat in the sun drinking coffee and wondering whether to wait an hour for the down bus at five or launch myself downwards on foot. But should I ever get there? Eleven kilometres by road and there were many *raccourcis* but should I find them in this fading misty light? The bus man told us how '*une bonne vieille femme*' had stumbled and broken her leg and lain there two hours in the rain, undiscovered. Not knowing if I was being cowardly or courageous I started down on foot – a rough stony path with steps. Once off and quickly losing height through lovely wooded mountain country (what would Julia say?),[1] I was glad I had, and snatched a few

[1]   She had iron rules about landscapes – wooded mountains were absolutely taboo.

flowers, spider orchids, campanula, as I went. Getting down it became harder to see the way and I got back in a little under two hours, not tired at all – and rather pleased with myself.

February 18th

Time is crawling, almost at a standstill; and I too have got into a clinch, like a bicycle with its wheels at right-angles and feel I'm about to topple over. A general running-down. Endurance somehow or other is the best I can set before myself – tough, intractable, wooden stuff it is, too.

Sometimes I imagine I have been undergoing a long, long surgical operation or series of operations. 'Yes, I'm afraid we must remove one arm, one leg, part of your side. Yes, the whole amputation will be done at one go but there will be a long subsequent stage of minor operations sealing off nerves and arteries, grafting new skin, cauterizations. Painful? Yes, very, I'm afraid, but nothing can be done about it; you must just hold tight to this bar when the pain gets unbearable, bite on the bullet. Prognosis? Well, your life will be limited, of course, but it will be life of a sort.'

A feeble attempt at 'fighting back' last night was not a great success. Had dinner earlier and walked off into the town, to cinema or casino I wasn't sure. One thing I did enjoy was the beauty of Old Menton by night – long golden-brown streaks like fine corduroy lying on the inky gelatinous water: the palm trees lit from below were a vivid acid green colour like painted tin ones in a child's tropical set: the beautiful church floodlit. But the film was so bad that I came away before the long programme was over, and as for the Casino it seems quite dead, except that during the interval the audience dashed out and staked a few francs. The croupiers weren't really paying attention, and gave people whatever they asked; there was no excitement.

February 20th

I'm inordinately surprised that I seem to see my situation so clearly and in such detail, like a view seen through a very clean windowpane. Ever since Ralph died that has been so, and it's never different, even in dreams. It's as if 'total eclipse' had brought 'total

35

awareness' going right down through all my submerged layers. Unaccountably though, yesterday was definitely better, and I don't quite understand why 'total awareness' doesn't bring a little more control. Anyway, I pegged through yesterday looking neither to right nor left, and as I write this date today I tell myself my deliverance from this special hell isn't far off. Only to move into another, of course; but I hope the discipline of this solitude has made for some strengthening-up of invisible weak joints.

My telephone calls from Mrs Stewart-Mackenzie have reached fever-pitch. She rings up every day and I never understand more than half of what she says.

February 23rd

'Discipline' is the answer, I believe, to the question that foggily arises often in my mind: What in God's name am I doing here? I'm trying by means of disciplinary mental gymnastics and rest combined to learn a technique for leading my new life. I faintly hope that practice and exercise will strengthen unused muscles, and teach me a few of the sort of 'tips' my alcoholics get by with.

Something has made me think very much more kindly of this hotel and Madame in particular. A little sandy old lady (English) about two feet high has been seen around lately, and I noticed Madame being very kind and ushering her about and taking her in the lift. This afternoon I was waiting for the lift when it descended with this little lady, all alone, wearing only thin white knickers under her jacket. She'd forgotten to put on her skirt. Madame hurried forward, so did someone else; with real kindness they took her up again, soothed her. Madame told me she had been with them fifteen years, all the year round, and was now ninety-six. She was senile, hardly understood what was said, and had recently been ill; but her daughter would do nothing for her and she wouldn't go to a *Maison de Santé*. 'So we look after her; but I can never go out. I have to be always ready to go to her,' she said with no tone of grievance, only a kind, bright look. She must be a really nice good woman.

February 25th

Suddenly this French episode, like the last phase of the eclipse, is rushing to its conclusion. My hands are already tightening a little (as I foretold) around my prison bars. The shadow of the world to come was thrown on my page by two letters from Craig[1] in answer to a vague one asking him how much money he thought I would have and whether he agreed I must sell Ham Spray His conclusion is £1,300 a year, after deduction of tax. However, as he calculates £3,000 as Ham Spray's selling price, i.e. probate valuation, which is *insane*, I'm wondering if he isn't going to be quite a hindrance rather than a help. I awoke in the small hours indignant and sat up in bed doing sums, and also wondering whether really money trouble wouldn't finally and absolutely destroy any desire to persist.

I spent the night before this money-infested one with the Lairdess[2] – Madeline, I'm supposed to call her. She picked me up after lunch at Peyronnet (Clive's villa), thought nothing of Little Barbara – Clive had gone to bed – and whisked me off into Italy, talking all the way. She often leaps several thoughts and lands on a stepping-stone far away, so that the intervening space must be guessed-at, yet I wonder that she isn't more tiring to be with.

March 1st

I think of England like a chess-board and want to know the position of the various pieces. Mary's absence from Stokke for so long is a loss for me. What of Robert? Last night at the Belle Escale restaurant Clive had 'a pain', turned white, panicked, got a frightened little boy expression and 'thought he felt sick'. Having safely got out of his plaster yesterday and been told his leg is completely healed, he now clings to his 'pain'. Barbara has only to leave him for five minutes and he begins muttering to himself, 'I don't know where BARbara's got to, I'm sure.' Soon afterwards he's calling 'BARBARA!' in exactly the same voice as a child calling 'NANNIE!'

---

[1] Macfarlane, my solicitor and dear old friend.
[2] Clive's name for Mrs Stewart-Mackenzie, who turned out to be 'the Mackenzie of Mackenzie', head of the clan.

Barbara and I drove to Castellar yesterday and as my sympathy for her in this state of things had acted like a poultice reducing the inflammation of irritation, I thought I'd try and do as Raymond suggested and 'help'.

Castellar is a wonderful place, standing on an island – seeming to float on a Turkish carpet in the middle of a deep valley with high mountains surrounding it. Though a rough wind blew at Menton, here it was perfectly still and warm, with the air sweet and fresh.

Company at the Hotel des Anglais is deteriorating – we now have two bishops and their wives (one like an ageing actor, posturing, egocentric, neurotic) and a large party of jolly gambling golfers who play 'I spy with my little eye' after dinner.

March 4th

The day after Barbara and I had gone to Castellar, which I fell so in love with, we took Clive there to lunch – a great success, excellent lunch (*poulet chasseur*), eaten in hot sun. The *patron*'s jokes at the expense of Clive, whom he described as an 'old carcass', trying to live up to his two wives (Barbara and me) seemed a touch macabre, but Clive didn't appear to mind, presumably because they were in French. I decided to walk down, lost my way and plunged over a rough hillside which soon became a precipice down which I slid and scrambled – worth it because there suddenly flashed on my dazzled eyes a field of brilliant red anemones (*fulgens*) waving in the sage-green shadow of the olives. A deeply moving sight. This I put together with the pleasure I got from a bus-drive twenty miles inland next day to Sospel, a mountain village standing on a river in a wide basin. Here all was far behind Menton – coconut-matting grass, only the earliest signs of spring, but going for a walk by a stream I found many banks covered with primroses and violets, great clumps of blue hepatica and spring squill. If I get (as I here undoubtedly do) my greatest solace from the visual aspect of nature, isn't it madness to try and live in London? Such places as Castellar and Sospel with their limpid air and clear light bringing out every roughness of wall surface, dent my mind profoundly and give me the support and sustenance that religion gives some people.

I woke yesterday feeling haunted and nightmarish. Perhaps

because the *mistral* was blowing, whisking up the sea into white crests. Perhaps because I dreamt vividly (but with muted emotional tone) of Ham Spray and was in 'our' bedroom as I must think of it, gazing at the bed and its two pillows. I knew in my dream that Ralph had had an appalling heart-attack, but was still alive. And still in this muted emotional mood, I *knew* that he would die very soon.

March 5th

What permanent effect do the surroundings in which one experiences violent or deep emotion have on one's mind? This place has bitten deeply into mine, leaving me with impressions that are superficially beautiful and soothing, like the great wide black grin of the bay edged with shining teeth, the gently-heaving water dimly seen by moonlight, yet have a sort of mocking irony about them. I don't think I shall ever want to come here again. There are other sounds and sights, like the comic, slow, gentle grunting rise or fall of the lift in this hotel, which makes me even now want to laugh and cry together.

The Graham Sutherlands came to see Clive and Barbara a few days ago, and yesterday invited Barbara and me to have a drink in their villa on the Castellar road. Here were human beings at last – who made the magistrates, bishops and retired businessmen in my hotel seem like zebras and camels. Graham Sutherland is an interesting, inscrutable man with curiously penetrating eyes, a good forehead, and the face of a writer or don rather than a painter. I guessed at his lower-class origins but found myself stumped for other clues. Kathy his wife is a handsome Irish Japanese-doll, friendly, funny, and very likeable.

Only four days left here and they look like being full, which is a jolly good thing.

March 7th

Yes, full they have been. Lunch with an old patron of the arts, Mrs Behrens.[1] Yesterday Phil and Phyllis Nichols[2] came for the day.

---

[1] She and her husband supported Stanley Spencer and commissioned the chapel near Newbury, perhaps his best work.

[2] Sir Philip Nichols, ex-Ambassador, and his wife who was our refugee with her children at the beginning of the War.

I have existed – somehow – now for three months without Ralph. Bob Gathorne-Hardy said, 'Think in terms of one day only; you *can* always manage a day more.' It is exactly the instructions given in my translation (*Alcoholics Anonymous*) for curing oneself of drink.

The Nicholses were very nice and friendly, Phyllis looking handsome and no older. Phil attacked me with questions about the future of Ham Spray, with a directness I liked. The Lairdess was in the lounge when I got back, along with five friends all now staying at this hotel. They are oh so jolly and friendly, Admirals, Generals and Honourables, and oh so dull. I have devised ways of *not* going through the lounge (it's full of English now, and *how* they shout and drawl both at once): instead I take the lift up one floor, then crab it along sidewise and down again to my little womb, the *salle d'écrire*. The smug, exhibitionist English voices reached me all the same, quacking on with their unimaginative implications that everyone is so civilized and can never be taken by surprise, that there are no such things as death, cancer, atom bombs, unhappy love or madness.

March 8th

Tomorrow I go! leave hold of my bars, throw myself off the cliff. Yesterday I had a visit from Eddie Gathorne-Hardy wearing a bright mustard-coloured shirt. He sat in the hotel garden astonishing the English by remarking loudly: 'It's my FUCKING brother,[1] my dear.' When going on to speak of his financial troubles he suddenly gulped and was silent. Could he be crying? I didn't dare trust my senses and pat his hand. It seemed incredible, but of course he was, and a few minutes later he took off his spectacles, brought out a large white handkerchief and mopped away the tears. Not having really absorbed the facts, and anyway not sympathizing with his attitude that the world is beastly unkind in not supporting him financially for doing nothing, my heart remained cold, my mind wandering and a small wave of emotional distaste rose momentarily up like heartburn within me. The lovable old scholar and lover of literature and the arts was still there however, and I enjoyed his company in a way. It *was* company. He hopes

[1] Lord Cranbrook ('Jock'), who had refused his request for more money.

to touch Mrs Howard, mother of Brian, for a large sum before going to Greece, in spite of busting her car to the tune of £180 last time he visited her. Did he hope to touch me? I don't think so.

Meanwhile John Banting,[1] genial slow old duck that he is, was visiting Barbara and Clive at the villa.

Coming out of the restaurant after dinner into the black sparkling night I was struck with pleasure-pain, a cool-warmth of emotion. This great beauty, which because of the psychological state it impinges on in me, seems always like a crust, has lain all round me for weeks and weeks. It has been in a way my best friend here. Yet I can do nothing with it; it washes over me like a very small wave, leaving me as I was before, a changeless unabreacted lump. Walked very slowly back to the hotel (dreading the *five* friends of the Lairdess likely to be in the lounge), alone, alone, ALONE. My independence, such as it is, gives me a meagre feeling of pride, and rears up like a thin unpleasant cobra. I am aware of the usual mixture of confidence and lack of it. Given propitious circumstances and a limited space of time I know I can get on with people like the Lairdess and the Sutherlands. I found a note from Kathy Sutherland begging me to stay a night longer as 'Kenneth Clark was longing to meet me'. Thank heavens I can't; this is only the result of Raymond's kind advocacy, and he would certainly have found me a disappointment.

March 9th

The last morning here. Yesterday I walked uphill between the two graveyards to lunch with Madeline Stewart-Mackenzie. Attractive little meal set on a table out of doors under a sweet-scented white buddleia, just freshly out and covered with butterflies. As I walked down again and looked at the steep terraces above the town, silent and still in the everlasting sunshine and a motionless haze, they reminded me of the illustrations to *Paradise Lost* in the copy I knew as a child, with the different levels of heaven, hell and purgatory, delicately detailed but bathed in mist. Purgatory is what they represent to me; and I feel when I think of the future like someone who's been holding their breath under water for a long,

---

[1] Surrealist painter.

long time and now – about to draw a fresh one – isn't quite sure what will come pouring into their lungs.

I set to and started sorting letters, packing, and now I must embark on the next terrace of my purgatory.

March 12th: Paris

I'm sitting up in my soft bed in Derek Jackson's flat, (rue Louis-David) with white satin quilted headpiece, hand-embroidered sheets, the long window curtained by huge botanical prints. Decanted into Paris two mornings ago, I have tumbled resistless as a twig into the swirling current. Derek is like a good-natured little boy, with his occasional apoplectic outbursts of boasting; he went back to England yesterday, and here I am alone with Anne and Heywood. Mary[1] left the same afternoon I arrived, having acted as a general in moving her pieces firmly on the board (the Hills are here to keep me happy and sane). 'I'm so happy,' she said. I asked her why. She didn't really know, except that she 'has a suitor in every port' and sufficient exciting journeys and invitations if they should fail.

Went to a cocktail party on Friday night, given by Ginette Spanier[2] and her husband. The Hills and I amalgamated with it rather poorly. Every woman that arrived went to the arms of every man and was held, kissed, cherished in public yet formal style. Our host and hostess had some inner source of overflowing warmth. Their guests were an American just back from Japan, Nancy Spain,[3] and a bald Frenchman with a fixed grin. Ginette Spanier whirled around us, high spirits sparking from her. Everything was wonderful; we were all marvellous in our sheltered cocoon world; confidence, blinkers, *simplisme*. Very French and very far from our style of life. We had reached the flat by a typical Parisian lift – wobbly, open-work and only made for three passengers. Anne refused to trust herself in it and took the stairs.

---

[1] Campbell.
[2] *Directrice* of Pierre Balmain.
[3] Writer.

When I asked Ginette if it ever broke down she said, 'Oh yes,' and went on to describe arriving home at 2 a.m. one cold winter's night when it stuck and no-one was left in the building to hear their shouts for help all night long.

March 14th

D-day, I must cross to England; though of course it's Ham Spray that is the great, terrible, unknown shock I must now face. Will it have been softened by all these intermediate stages – Menton, Paris, London? The Hills and I had two nights here alone and then last night they both left. I've not 'done' much in Paris. Went to the Berthe Morisots and the Musée Jaquemart-André in which the Exhibition stands. On Sunday – a lovely day – went with the Hills and three *jeune filles en fleur* (Harriet[1] and two friends from her finishing-school) to a park on the outskirts and lunched there. The girls were very charming; they varied from worldly sophistication to infinite childishness, buying balloons and saying, 'God, how exciting!'

Yesterday afternoon Harriet and I went to the Balmain show, and were mesmerized by watching tall thin girls walk towards us like giraffes, turn, twist and giraffe-it back again – keeping their expression unaltered throughout their long ordeal. General impression – not much imagination except in evening clothes, but sumptuous materials, rich bright unsubtle colours and impeccable cut.

Now I must get up and face the climb to the next terrace of purgatory.

March 16th: England, Lambourn

Fidelio last night with Janetta was almost unbearably moving. The music poured over the frozen substitute for a human being that I now am, and violently thawed it – a painful process, because some feelings deliberately crushed under tombstones turned in their

---

[1] Elder daughter of the Hills.

43

graves, and the blood painfully ran into them as pins and needles do into limbs.

I had too many people to confront in London, too many stock-brokers and lawyers in particular. A long session with Craig, which at the time seemed satisfactorily lucid and practical but has left behind a deathly sense of unreality. Then I took refuge with the Gowings in the country.

Lawrence came into my room yesterday and made me a speech of extraordinary kindness, which brought tears of gratitude to my eyes, saying that I was the only person who didn't 'interfere with their spiritual life' and they wanted me to come as much as I liked. He then lent me his car to drive to Ham Spray, and Julia came too.

Well – Ham Spray – there it was, extraordinarily the same as it has stood and looked through all sort of tragedies, moods, personal dramas, and the successive deaths of Lytton, Carrington and Ralph. Houses are impassive things, more like great rocks in the middle of a waterfall than man-made creations. It didn't look or feel to me haunted, nor did I expect to see Ralph at every moment – as Janetta did when she returned there. It merely seemed dead. And though it's as near being my home as anywhere at the moment, it didn't magnetize me; it wasn't a living organism at all – just walls, books going mouldy, and a piano whose keys stuck when I touched them. Craig wants me to set about selling it at once; there was pressure from Noel[1] too, and I suppose they are right – but I feel hustled. I saw Mrs Hoare,[2] and Wilde[3] – who had just two things he wanted to say, both egocentric: that he would like to have the first refusal of buying his cottage, and that the agricultural wages had gone up since January 1st.

Monday morning

I woke at six-thirty and heard the proletarian voices of workers going to Harwell, and later the cloppity-clop of race-horses (so exciting a noise that I scuttled out of bed to look). Each morning I begin my mono-dialogue, to adopt Unamuno's absurd word,

---

[1] Carrington, one of Ralph's executors, and his brother-in-law.
[2] Our village daily.
[3] The gardener.

the subject of which may be Julia and Lawrence, my loneliness, Napoleon III (about whom I'm reading). If I wake in the night there are words, not pictures running through my head.

All yesterday Lawrence and Julia concentrated on their 'spiritual life' while I spread my papers all over the broad table looking onto the garden, and pegged away at my 'work' – my life-belt. A short walk by myself trying to project my hypothetical existence into a small country house on these green rolling hills, not very satisfactorily. I passed stable-lads with short thin legs bowed round invisible horses walking out with taller girls with thick purple bare ones stuffed into patent leather, stiletto-heeled shoes; the horse-civilization of bungalows topped by huge television aerials, smooth lawns and glossy cars. The cold wind blew as I walked out later with Julia. She had come bemused with work from a good session at her writing, and with writer's problems hanging in clouds around her. So that was what we mainly talked of, walking through the woods, beside clumps of half-frozen white violets drooping from limp stalks.

March 24th: Montpelier Square[1]

The London mincing-machine has been mashing me pretty fine, even though I retire to my bedroom and work. I can just face it in the mornings; at night – struggling in a bus to visit Raymond at Canonbury, say – I hardly can.

And Time rolls on. The fact that my superficially consolidated state has no firm foundation is brought home to me in various ways – such as the partial thawing that *Fidelio* brought, and my sometimes violent reaction to other people, of whom Lord knows I've had lately more than I can take. Meeting and greeting them with a fictitious mildness and submission, I suddenly find a fierce resistance fending-off their approaches. 'No, *you* aren't what I want, *you*'re offering me an ersatz substance. TAKE IT AWAY!'

March 29th: Ham Spray

I have passed my first night here. 'Our' bed has become 'my' bed and I have faced the great shock of return, which in fact produced

[1] Janetta's London house.

45

an overwhelming gush of affection for the dear place, '*this* is my home', 'I belong here', and this in spite of my firm determination to leave it.

I spent my first nights here with Janetta and Burgo for company. After that, alone with Maria and Rose[1] tucked away upstairs, my heart thumped, panic seized me and I took to whiskey, watching the clock tick past till I could decently go to bed. I have a feeling that the longer I stayed here, the more the friendliness of the house would become a comforting support to be leant on rather than adding to my sense of deprivation. So I now hope the whirring wheels set going by house-agents and buyers may allow me to stay here on and off throughout the summer. They ring me up, squabble about 'sole rights' like dogs over a bone, and one, a pale schoolmistress from Thake and Paginton has already been to see it, and didn't bat an eyelid at £9,500.

'Fill every moment' is still my motto, and there's been no difficulty so far. Typescript of *Alcoholics Anonymous* to correct and send off. Sample of *Zoubeida* to translate. Endless house organization, food ordering. Rose likes to spend some time with me, and Maria sinks into her detective stories.

March 31st, Good Friday

Translating most of the day in an empty, lonely house, Rose and Maria having left on the early train. Thake and Paginton's clients are to come and see the house on Monday and with the possibility they might buy it I'm faced with the future – NOWHERE, or tied to poor Janetta's tail, such a kind sensitive tail, too. But I know my solution must include peace, privacy and above all, *independence*. I cannot substitute any other dependence for what I've lost, and feel I must take that, with all the horrors of loneliness involved. I explained this to Lawrence and he understood me more than Julia did, who read me a lecture as vivid as she could make it on the horrors of loneliness. As if I didn't know them!

A fever possesses me at times when I think of moving out and constructing my life elsewhere, and look round at all the millions and millions of 'things' clutching at me with their dense cloud of associations and asking me to decide: keep or destroy.

[1] Janetta's Spanish maid, and youngest daughter Rose Jackson.

April 1st

The house is now rather full – Janetta, both children and Maria, Burgo, and comings and goings from Kees, Hendersons,[1] Gowings. But this very approximation of the life of the past makes its essential differences startlingly plain, and I remember the glorious uproarious laughter of the past. Have just had an interesting, human and sympathetic conversation with Burgo, but which has given me a sight of his own drifting state. Very adult, very acute, very intelligent but full of undischarged love and therefore not happy.

Sometimes I think of a *complete* upheaval – to live abroad.

April 2nd, Easter Day

Nicko came to dinner last night. We talked of religion, and an argument developed from my saying that we who believe in good and beauty are ultimately accepting something on faith alone, just as the religious do. Nicko wanted to deny this but didn't have his reasons ready though seemingly enjoying the argument. Janetta brought up, more reasonably, the fact that there were numerically *more* acts of faith in religion. With a pink patch on her cheek, she said she could never possibly marry someone who was a believer, and hinted that it was morally *wrong* to do so. Also that she didn't believe in marriage. I didn't enquire whether she meant the religious ceremony or lifelong companionship.

April 4th

Potential buyers of Ham Spray came yesterday afternoon, a day of soaking drizzle, the downs invisible. I liked the man – an honest, ex-RAF type; also two friendly and musical little girls. They spent a long time here and I think were 'interested', only time will show how much. When the time of their expected visit arrived, my heart beat so painfully I felt I should die of it. As usual, calm came with the start of the ordeal.

Today the skies still weep in utter silence. I have been rung up by various friends, Rachel[2] asking me to stay – nice that – and

---

1   Nicko and Mary.
2   Lady David Cecil.

just now Bunny Garnett. They have heard I'm here and their motive is entirely friendly. Burgo left for three nights this morning. He has been kind, sweet and helpful to me, but I'm not happy about him . . . I am now alone in the house. I feel as though I were surrounded by grey ash and that the less I look about me, the better.

April 5th

The sun gleams sideways from the west onto our lawns, and such a magic has returned to the garden that I'm swelling and bursting with indignation at the two tough beefy men (Harrods and Neates) who have just been tramping through and through it everywhere, and depreciating it for all they're worth in strident voices, till it seems as though only a lunatic could want to take over this Paradise from me. £6,750 is all they propose to ask. 'No-one would want the house' was their line, only its 'position' – and by that they meant 'the favoured Newbury area', *not* the wonderful seclusion, ravishing surroundings and view. A fierce desire to keep it came over me, resentment of their coarse male violation, and lack of appreciation.

April 11th

Yesterday three lots of viewers came to see the house in pouring rain and plugged round in macintoshes and gumboots. Burgo supported me gallantly. An offer at £8,000 'take it or leave it' was telephoned through by Craig in the afternoon. Not yet, I said – for £9,500 is the price I had asked. After nine the telephone rang. It was the agent who had sent all the viewers: 'I've got good news for you. I've sold your house, and at the full price.' Murmuring approval, I felt my heart drop like a stone, and from then on the agony swelled and swelled, and Burgo was even more upset than I, and retired to the music-room to play *When I am laid in earth* on the gramophone. I went up to bed feeling I was a murderer and had killed Ham Spray with my own hands. Struggles to keep equilibrium and rational thoughts going were defeated by emotional sounds from Burgo below who was drowning his feelings in whiskey, bangs, 'Fuck!' shouted aloud, and other remarks into the void; tramping feet to and fro in the music-room. Somehow the night was got through, though not improved by Mrs Edginton, the buyer, ringing up and asking if she might 'come and see *our* house again tomorrow. Just poke about a bit, you know?'

Oh, God! Vanessa[1] has died and Morgan[2] has had a heart attack.

p.m. They, the harmless viewers, are back. My house isn't my own. That is, I don't feel I can go up and sprawl full length on my bed as I should like. I sit alone in the music-room, tense and pretty near the end of my tether. How endurable is it going to be, living here these months ahead? Will it be like living with a husband who has told one he is going to leave and set up with someone else?

They are prodding holes in the rotten floors, and no doubt finding all sorts of horrors. If they won't have the house after all I shall have the struggle to do all again. Meanwhile I sit here on red-hot nails of restlessness, finding it impossible to concentrate on anything. I wonder if there's any book in existence which would hold my attention.

April 12th

Righting my position gradually. One thing that helped was the arrival of two more buyers called Elwes, who appreciated the house for what it is and therefore endeared themselves to me sufficiently for me to ask them in and offer them sherry. They seemed dead keen, and determined to oust Colonel Edgington if they could.[3] As the Colonel and his lady had gone off very markedly *not* looking me in the eye, I felt (as now transpires) that might be easy.

April 14th

I wish I could sometimes write about things that are delightful or beautiful and not only the twists of the screw on my rack. There *are* such moments, but the others swamp them, and twisting and turning like a rabbit pursued by dogs I just look about for relief, for some way out.

[1] Vanessa Grant.
[2] E.M. Forster.
[3] The Elweses signed the contract shortly after this, and it is symptomatic that I didn't record the fact in my diary.

I suppose I shall get through somehow. Peace and quiet and no responsibilities are what I long for; even telephoning the shops and giving orders to the staff are almost more than I can bear. The advent of James and Alix[1] and Janetta's friend the Duke of Devonshire tomorrow seem like great cliffs. I think *I* shall like *him* but how could anyone like the crazy obsessional ghost I have become?

April 15th

All the visitors have arrived. I like Andrew Devonshire very much; in his voluble speech and a strange sliding backwards 'chassis' movement he reminds me very much of David.[2] Like David, too, he comes to meet one, sees what one means, and responds to it. He's interested in lots of things, from politics to fritillaries.

Before his arrival I already felt worn out by six hours' steady talking to James and Alix, delightful though they were. Alix in particular was in magnificent vein, stately in her fur coat and helmet hat, describing how she had 'advertised in the agony column of *The Times* for a movable artificial tree on *wheels* and got twenty-one replies'. She thinks now of advertising for two 'miniature bowling screens to keep off the draught'!

Burgo very sweet to me. Colonel Elwes *seems* to want the house.

Now it's all over and I sit in the sun on the lawn, rooks cawing. Waking after a long sleep to this beautiful day, a wave of sadness came over me because I was selling the house, and I had to bring up my regiments of reasoned argument to face it with.

April 18th: Cranborne

Slept as I have not done since returning to Ham Spray in the Cecils' spare bed. A letter from Boris[3] imploring me not to leave Ham Spray upset me greatly: 'I read your letter with the greatest sorrow in my heart. To abandon the house where you lived so long and where happy memories supersede the sad ones is a terrible uproot-

---

[1] Strachey.

[2] Cecil, his uncle.

[3] Anrep, the eminent Russian mosaicist, whose works embellish the National Gallery, the Tate, the Bank of England, Westminster Cathedral and many other buildings in London and elsewhere.

ing of your life. Is it wise? The unhappiness you feel now will mellow with time, and happy days of many years will come back in watching Burgo and his friends, and your old friends, gathering round under the roof which for all of us is a centre of loving hospitality and enlightenment and the greatest English civilized taste in all things. To ruin all this will be a disaster for all of us and primarily for you and Burgo . . .' and there was lots more in this vein. David was reassuringly firm on the other side. Now I have eased up for a space and sailed into an inland sea of relaxation and half-wittedness, shot with currents of *angst* so disconnected that they seem like lunacy. But I loved the delightfully communicative and articulate family atmosphere last night, with Jonathan (aged twenty-one) in his red velvet jacket and Laura in pyjamas and dressing-gown. Jonathan talks lovingly and freely to both his parents, and is a visibly sweet character, with very long sensitive fingers.

Yesterday evening under the tall bare trees full of cawing rooks, Rachel took me to see a little thatched cottage in the village, thoroughly and tastelessly done up. It was useful only to show me how I *couldn't* live, but struck no pang (as I think kind Rachel feared it might) with a vision of loneliness. Because *quite impossible.*

April 19th

The quick sensitiveness and response of the whole Cecil family is delightful. Crying off a visit to Constantine FitzGibbon's last night I was talked to for nearly two hours by Laura (age thirteen) about school 'crushes' and 'pashes' – *not* the same – and all the 'notes' and 'tears' that accompany them. She unpacked for me too her thoughts and plans about going to boarding-school next term, how she would be careful not to be too eager to answer questions in class, 'hold herself in', 'refrain from making bad jokes which I'm rather given to' and so on. All these confidences to a practically strange old person were flattering and entertaining. She's very unusual in her quick projection of her thoughts into words. It's a little the same with Jonathan. Articulacy is a family habit, and there is enormous charm, like that of a flourishing garden, in the Cecils' spontaneous family life and freely flowering sympathy, interest and love for each other.

April 20th

Today I leave this kind sheltering roof. I strolled with David yesterday through the gardens of the other two Cecilian houses in the village – the beautiful Manor House belonging to Lord Cranborne, and Lord Salisbury's red-brick Georgian one. Spots of rain fell between the flowering cherries (dazzlingly pretty in spite of their tasteless combination of flower and leaf colour). A Shakespearian clown with a thick black wig was cutting logs with a tearing dental sound. The comfortable secure class-conscious civilization of the past lay around us as we discussed the tendency to 'depression' of the young today. Both Jonathan and Hugh (who arrived today from Lismore, very cheerful and amusing in MacCarthy style), say that their friends suffer from this depression. David likes to ignore the black side of things and wanted to belittle it; last night Jonathan again repeated it. He put it down to dread of war and so many having done military service – which gave me a momentary pleasure as at seeing a sum done correctly. It is so very logical. Much argument about capital and corporal punishment last night, wherein I found myself in complete agreement with Jonathan and so was naturally impressed by his intelligence. Rachel wavered, and it was David who with considerable emotion defended the diehard view, while constantly saying with a smile: 'I don't know what I'm arguing about – I really agree with you. I used not to but I do now.' He has an emotional dislike of the new 'rational' or 'moral' approach to punishment – surely it's odd to use such words as terms of reproach? – and stoutly maintained that nine out of ten boys would prefer being beaten to having to 'build a wall' – the most boring task he could think of. Everyone brought up their guns against him. Jonathan, to whom it was closer, vividly described the morbid and terrifying atmosphere before a beating at Eton, when all the younger boys were confined to their rooms and the prefects stalked through the corridors swishing their canes. David was surrounded and cut off and ultimately defeated by us all, and he didn't take it altogether smoothly.

April 24th

(In the train from Wivenhoe[1] to London)

Amazed and horrified at the relentless passage of time, the long white empty lengthening stretch of life without Ralph in it. That's why friends tell the bereaved to *hang on* and the time will pass. It does, all too fast, carrying one further and further away from the only real happiness, before one has the strength even to clasp the painful memory of that happiness close and be sure it never hazes over. I see Ralph shooting off, away, back, through an infinity of empty space like a star on its orbit, and must submit to his flight. I am astonished by this long blank bit of my solitary life and dread it should be prolonged so that my thirty-five years with him might seem not the whole of my life but a part, in shocking falsity of emphasis.

All yesterday Dicky and Denis drove me through the flat featureless landscape, which even bright new leaves and apple-blossom couldn't make attractive. To see Ickworth, Mildenhall Church, lots of lovely little towns with houses behind whose square windows one could easily have lived, were they anywhere else.

We dined out with a huge cavalcade of Nicholses on Saturday – also Irene,[2] and Vivien John[3] solidly beautiful with husband and two plump boys.

April 27th: Montpelier Square

Supper last night with Julia and Lawrence in their Percy Street flat, eating a frozen Woolworth meal out of foil dishes (no washing-up, choice of three sorts); much laughter, altogether delightful.

My red and grey room at the top of the house is a haven, but has become full of my own sadness so that the air seems opaque with it.

Last night here; packing up. This evening I talked to Nicky[4] and

---

[1] Where I had been staying with the artists Richard (Dicky) Chopping and
     Denis Wirth-Miller. Dicky and I had been engaged for many years on
     an abortive British Flora, he as illustrator, I as writer.
[2] Lady Gater, Phil's elder sister.
[3] Youngest daughter of Augustus John.
[4] Janetta's oldest daughter.

53

ate a schoolgirl's supper with her in the kitchen. Much enjoyed this: why didn't I do it before?

These London days of looking at houses and flats have brought me very little but dislike of the ugliness and noise and hectic confusion of this town. Walking along Victoria Street, among worried pale jostling faces, seeing nothing that wasn't hideous, I longed to get away and hide, turn my face to the wall. (Yet, most of the time I see that my only hope is to be here.) I was on my way from the Roman Catholic Cathedral to see Boris putting up his mosaics. Plunged into the great dark place with its high walls and domes of brick sooty as Euston Station, and after wandering past a few devout kneelers or candle-lighters I heard unmistakable voices softly speaking Russian behind a boarded-off chapel marked No Admittance. Boris looked ill and sad, a magnificent crumbling ruin among what he believes to be his last works. I was staggered by their size: huge saints and apostles go right to the ceiling and their large Jewish faces and enormous black eyes stared at me as I climbed ladder after dusty wobbling ladder right to the barrel roof, where Italian workmen were putting up a round motif. Impressive, huge, yet I didn't altogether like it. It seemed to lack some of Boris' subtlety and poetry, the colossal hands and feet were clumsy. Then a brilliantly-conceived lamb about to be sacrificed, or a snake or a bowl of fruit caught my eye and charmed me.

I was painfully moved by talking to Boris, by the recollection of his letter begging me not to leave Ham Spray and by anxiety about his mosaics there.

A social evening with Cyril,[1] Diana Witherby, Julian Jebb and Magouche,[2] who is like Janetta in a lower, warmer key. Together they remind me of the duet for soprano and mezzo in Verdi's *Requiem* – the 'black-edged paper' as Desmond Shawe-Taylor describes it. She's the only person I ever met who seems at all like Janetta. I like her thick dark hair, low rich voice, warm smile and large eyes. In fact, she's very attractive indeed.

In the train back to poor dear Ham Spray. My own shipwreck has filled me with terror and amazement at the mortal danger run so serenely day after day by anyone who loves anyone else. Yet they calmly buy tooth-paste and plan for weeks and months ahead,

[1] Connolly.
[2] Phillips, later Fielding.

just as I did, with heaven knows less justification than most. It's the only way to live, yet it seems patently insane.

May 10th: Ham Spray

Here I have been now two nights. Burgo arrived to keep me company, his own idea. He is pleased (and so am I) because he's been given the job of film critic to *Time and Tide*.

Today suddenly spring (summer almost) burst over us. My present task, which I've been hurling myself into since I got back, is sorting out James' books from mine – the first step in the pulling-down of the construction that is Ham Spray. Looking for more Lyttonian papers in the little closet next to the library, I came across some Carrington documents – the huge list of presents she left as an unsigned postscript to her Will, and a letter to Ralph left with it. Of course I've read them several times before, but this time in a new light. The letter, deeply moving and touching, yet had a strain of masterfulness – of wanting still to have control from *outre tombe* which I remember Ralph resented at the time. She wanted him to '*promise* always to live at Ham Spray'. Well, he did live there – but I remember that I was surprised how almost cynical he was, in spite of his shattered state after both their deaths – because she still wanted to hold the reins, even while planning to renounce life. Her request that Tommy[1] should be commissioned to make a tombstone over her ashes in the shrubbery was the one he resented most violently.

He was, I realize now, being characteristically realistic. He felt very strongly that by choosing death regardless of other people's feelings, she had abnegated her right to control the lives of those friends – in particular himself and me. We were going to live in Ham Spray because it was his and we wanted to. We had decided to make our life there and we did so for nearly thirty happy years, but it would have been a different matter for us to live with a *memento mori* in the shape of a tombstone within the confines of our small garden. In his own Will, Ralph made no stipulation or request for me to live at Ham Spray. He was too rational not to see that this was *my* choice – and I have made it.

---

[1] Stephen Tomlin, sculptor, first husband of Julia Strachey.

May 25th

In glorious summer weather I dismantle my life and my past, accompanied in turn by Joan Cochemé, and now Isobel Strachey[1] and with much active help from Burgo. The business of taking these companions into a sort of ersatz married life is not as difficult as I had feared, just because it is in no way a simulacrum.

What is to be done about Boris's mosaic fireplaces when I leave? I had hoped to take away the one Boris made as a wedding-present for Ralph and me; but the tesserae of both had been hammered into the cement before it hardened, and the job would be difficult. I wrote to Boris about it but he is still hard at work in the Roman Catholic Cathedral, has been quite ill and must be over seventy. He begged me not to let any unqualified person attempt to do it. I talked to Mrs Elwes on one of their very tactful visits to their future home. She is a nice, civilized woman; she knew all about Boris's art but 'happened not to like it' and felt it wouldn't 'go' with her Chinese and other antiques. She has agreed to cover the fireplaces carefully and see that they are undamaged.

June 1st

Isobel has been here nearly a fortnight, drifting through the house, reading out the clues of crossword puzzles with incredible slowness, and then gazing out of the window trying to guess them with large sad eyes. She's very sweet and kind to me; I do hope it's not a great strain for her being here. Her company and conversation are like a diet of Bengers food and I enjoy it very much while still thinking longingly of the stimulating ox-tail soup I used to enjoy.

June 19th

After trudgery and drudgery unspeakable but bearable, I close this book before leaving for the North tomorrow.

---

[1] Both among my oldest and closest friends.

June 21st

In the train to Windermere, the unfamiliar landscape chug-chugging past. Six weeks of dismantling, destroying and coal-heaver exertion have left the inside of my head a watery white blank, anaesthetized and disintegrated into hundreds of pieces as small as those of a mosaic. Iris Murdoch's new book has at least one good sentence in it: 'How are you?' 'Dead, otherwise fine.' But such deadness is a mockery of the black velvet oblivion I dream about.

To see the Leningrad Ballet last night with Maud Russell, Raymond and Boris. Boris overtopped everyone with his distinction and charm, Raymond in his London mood, pedalling away on an invisible bicycle of contemporary culture – the latest in books, music, pictures. Myself dimly aware as in a dream of the technical skill of the dancers, and in particular of the fluency of their movements, like an effortless stream rather than a series of discreet gymnastics; soundless also. Unlike those of the thudding English, their feet fell like cats' paws after even a colossal bound. I was moved by one girl, Sizova, and her beautiful head-, neck- and waist-movements – otherwise as a spectacle it was tasteless.

June 26th: Skelwith Fold, Cumbria

Tom[1] and Nadine's solid house, freshly whitewashed and with slate slab floors, stairs and fireplaces of an intense blue-green-grey, looks out onto two gardens rampant with roses, foxgloves and ferns, and on one side through the bare stems of two firs to a small green mountain snugly fitted into its velvet turf, but with grey rocks coming through here and there. All my energies are geared to adaptation to my different hospitable environments. The effort is great and the prospect of change makes me quiver. I prune my own desires right back to the root, which results in an unreal subhuman state, with sudden geyserlike outbursts. Tom and Nadine are both very kind. I slept my drugged sleep in my little ground-floor bedroom or sat doing my translation on the window-ledge. Long walks, picnics every day, all beautiful and quite physically tiring. On the hottest day we toiled up to Stickle Tarn under Langdale Pikes and sat by the high steely sheet of water watching

---

[1] Marshall (my brother) and his wife.

climbers roped with nylon tackle the last rock face. The waterfalls between rocks covered in deep green moss, the astonishing cleanness, lack of anything hideous or vulgar; the quiet, sweet soft vegetable peace; the particular beauty of deciduous trees growing at the water's edge single or in groups – feasting on all this greenness and beauty has cast a temporary veil over my sharpest pangs.

June 29th: Kyle House, Skye[1]

Colin, Pin and I drove here yesterday, all day long, from cold austere handsome Edinburgh. Out of my window the strip of sea between Skye and the mainland lies silver under a dark grey sky, and small gaps of blue have searchlights of sun shooting from them. Both this house and Edinburgh are luxuriously comfortable and full of lovely things.

July 3rd

Absorbed by the business of adapting, I have written nothing, thought nothing, and now my stay in Skye is nearly over. Last night Colin took me and the weekend visitors (Smythes) a long drive along the coast after dinner, in a light that was neither day nor night, but such as you'd expect on the moon, cool and mysterious. Sea like pale watered silk, rippling in; the mountains towering up with magnificent suddenness yet insubstantial and grey-blue. They challenge, impose on one, cry out, 'Look at us', drag one's attention. The track growing ever rougher and smaller, and fields yellow-white (like the white hair of ex-blondes) with ox-eye daisies, ended in a low farm and a grassy slope covered with orchids going gradually to the sea. Oh, what peace! Mr Smythe (he calls it Smith) is a little bent seventy-year-old solicitor, with sharp humorous eyes like a Skye terrier. His trousers are braced up to almost under his chin and it's a pleasure to see a thought which amuses him dawning on his face. His wife balances her huge body on table-legs swelling out at the ankles. She's a 'good' woman, worthy, broad-minded, musical, and with an almost morbid interest in the troubles of others. She took me a drive, ostensibly to show off her car, but I

---

[1] The Mackenzies' house.

suddenly felt she had scented sorrow in me and wanted to draw it out like a vacuum-cleaner. I resisted.

This morning it rains – yet it's beautiful here beyond dreams, and soothing (though I'm not soothed, but palpitating with dread of the future). As we drove back after our night-drive the car wireless announced Hemingway's death 'accidentally' cleaning his gun. Lucky chap – or perhaps just brave, rational chap? – or selfish chap? How can one tell?

I dreamt very vividly that my dear silver bracelet (a present from Ralph) snapped ruggedly in half and I was staring in horror at the jagged break when a voice took me to task for being so selfish. Hadn't I noticed that the other half had flown through the air and cut the arm of a stranger, a harmless plump girl? A clear warning to keep in mind that my bereft state can cause pain indirectly to others too? A tip to be less self-absorbed?

Just now Mrs Smythe looked in to say goodbye. 'I do hope you'll soon feel better.' Illogically, I resent her intrusion and the implication that I have appeared as stricken as I feel, in spite of efforts, pills and God knows what.

July 5th

On I go again; in the train once more, dowsed into fictitious calm after a night of lying awake while the future put its face close and stared at me grimly. I'm trickling gently beside an arm of the sea; herons stand on the stony shore with their feet in the clean translucent water. Ghostly mountains, magically lit here by a flicker of sun, dark there. No houses; blessed lack of people. Surely one should embrace this impersonal balm the visible world gives one, and stop trying to make do with makeshift human contacts. I admired Colin and Pin's way of life, and have come away from Kyle House with increased affection for them both.

July 6th: Braham[1]

The screw twists where one doesn't expect it. This morning waking in comfort, a Scotch voice bringing my breakfast in bed inside the solid stone walls of the Lairdess' castle, Braham, why did I so soon

[1] Mrs Stuart-Mackenzie's house.

give way to nightmare feelings of panic and malaise? In desperation I walked off among the huge trees feeling I must surely die of sheer lack of desire to live if I lay down in the fine silky grass beneath them. The Lairdess is distracting to be with, scatty, asking the same question three times and not waiting for an answer, haring off at a tangent, inconsequential. My heart sank when she put forward a project for me to be her 'companion' in a house near Gibraltar. Oh, how can I escape? Where's the door? I feel like the reluctant bull in the bullfight I couldn't sit through at Mecina Bombaron. This project which she has been driving into me like a banderilla, makes my sense of unreality swell. It was a mistake to come here, I am so out of my element. I long to relax with some familiar person – Mary, Janetta, Julia, Raymond.

I cried off an afternoon expedition and lie on my bed, the stonewalled room having become a prison, the Lairdess my jailer. Hang on, hang on – but why? The only comfort I got in this waste of cowardice and seaweedy desolation was the sudden tiny welling-up of something I recognized as returning courage. I *won't* be beaten. Not yet anyway, without another try.

July 7th

Last night's dinner-party consisted of two Generals and (staying the night) a Colonel and his lady. Lord, how I longed for Ralph to discuss it with: 'slumming', he would have called it. I must somehow avoid getting so far out of my element again. But one General was quite charming; he'd been a prisoner of war in Italy and escaped with Carton de Wiart, and he was so deaf I suddenly realized that his formula, 'Yes, I *know*' meant he hadn't heard a thing. It was the Colonel's lady I found so repellent, with her euphoric self-satisfaction, and everyone she talked of 'a Poppet' or 'a Sweetie': so full of high spirits and conviction that everything's wonderful. It's NOT, you silly fool.

July 11th: Ham Spray

Back here with Janetta (very comforting and strong) and Burgo (in-turned and pacing). Now I'm near the end of two hard-working days almost alone (I'm sleeping at Stokke),[1] I suppose I've never been quite so alone, and I've not really minded it. All today sticking red and white tabs on furniture, telephoning, arranging, feverish.

With Janetta's encouragement I've decided to be off next Saturday week to join her in Austria, shortening this nightmarish uprooting process by a week; crack! – one by one the roots come out of the soil.

July 24th: Alpbach, Austria

Ham Spray is a closed book. I am here surrounded by nursing-home peace, and relieved of the ghastly pressure like a huge iron weight descending on me during these last weeks, surrounded also by a landscape which is curiously hideous and yet enjoyable, and with the delightful company of Janetta, Georgia Tennant and Rose. More I shall fill in later. At present just one thing: it's over. I'm here – away.

July 26th

Being here went bad on me for the first time, and the intensity of my loneliness rose up like a great iceberg. All yesterday Janetta and Georgia were away fetching Georgie[2] and Julian Jebb from Innsbruck. Rose and I played games, sitting in bathing suits on the hot balcony, walked to the village and swam, came back and cooked our lunch. A governessy sort of day with this dear little girl, who talked to me far from dully, about her first day at the Lycée and how she had cried and 'hated being deserted'.

We are living in a regular Tyrolean chalet of solid wood. At first sight I thought of them all as hideous, as the landscape is fundamentally; I've come round to the style in a *sort* of way – see its point, though it's not a point I like: the smell of the wood, the solid tables and cupboards and benches built into the walls, the fact that everything is so well-made. We look out on intersecting

---

[1] Mary Campbell's house, 6 miles away.
[2] Kee, Janetta's second daughter.

valleys, with too-close mountainy hills far too densely covered in crawling mats of pines. Little green plump alps appear here and there among these pines and on each is a chalet gazing out under its wide roof like a poke-bonnet or an ark. The village is nothing but hotels and tourist shops, full of hideously ugly German tourists: men like bloated beetles in shorts on skinny legs, fantastically fat women, all walking with an ungainly straddling waddle, propped on long sticks. The ambience is innocent, naive and goody-goody, *stupid*, jolly and wholesome. Very holy, too – one can't walk a yard without coming on Jesus on his cross.

For some days after I came it was cold, with ugly opalescent, gunmetal clouds hanging over the hills. Now suddenly a burning sun.

Georgia Tennant at twenty is remarkably mature and a delightful, intelligent, high-spirited girl. Tall and strong, with fine long plump limbs and a shock of darkish golden hair half veiling her round pussy-cat face. I like her enormously and she has been very nice to me. She's a passionate reader, enjoyer of jazz, avid for life, one of Lawrence's[1] students. She's highly responsive to her company. When Julian came, 'queer' though he obviously is, her face softened and broadened and caved in like a yielding sponge. Not so with Derek, here the first night, too old I suppose, though 'normal'.

Julian – what to say? He is euphoric, friendly, very articulate; he launches into imitations, crows with delight; everything seems to be SIMply delightful, his world full of BRILLiantly clever people and MARvellous books. But I like him very much.

No letters have come for me, I don't know why, and I have written none. Craving the amputation to be complete, so as to profit from perfect detachment from all the obsessional problems and commitments of the past, I resolve to concentrate on a few things such as books, flowers, translation, sleep.

Last night the usual thoughts of flight or withdrawal came crowding in: to a hotel in the village, home to England and heaven knows what. I know I must stick it out, but when the Campbells[2] come I think I should have to go anyway, and I dread Janetta

[1]   Gowing.
[2]   Robin, Susan and baby William.

trying, out of kindness, to take on too many of us here. No-one seems to have any notion of going, so I shall.

July 28th

Arthur Koestler and his 'secretary' Cynthia, known to him as Angel, live in a chalet like this one, a quarter of a mile away. They came in for a drink two nights ago, swaggering after climbing a mountain, Koestler dressed in the beetle-like Austrian uniform – shorts and long socks – yet speaking scornfully in what to us sounds a German accent of 'Krauts'. Conversation about this last night – Julian was shocked by it because he thought of Koestler as virtually a Kraut himself; I because I hate all those contemptuous national nicknames. Koestler has adopted Austrian civilization under his wing, and is galled that Janetta (one of the few people he respects) shouldn't appreciate it and the landscape. 'The peasants vould not like that. I think it is so vise of them,' he says, lecturing us about their way of life. Little Arthur's Austria may or may not be true to fact, but it doesn't attract me. He mentioned that the Wayland Youngs were coming here soon. 'I don't agree with his politics, but I like him,' he said. 'What are his politics?' I asked. 'Never mind that,' – running on quickly – (he doesn't listen to other people). I thought this unnecessarily snubbing and couldn't help saying: 'It would have been more interesting to know.'

Lovely evening walk after a hot afternoon, with Janetta and the children up the hillside. When one reaches the fringes of the hated pines one grows suddenly enamoured of them. I like the way the grass is smoothly spread between their trunks (no needly wastes as in England) and there are grey stones breaking through as well as grey stumps of old pines. Coolness and a scented peace wafts from them, horse-flies as well.

August 1st

Janetta and all the others went off on a jaunt to the Bromovskys[1] yesterday morning. Last night Rose, with whom I was alone, was sick and she has gone on being sick if she ate or drank anything all today. I seem to have been trying all day to mop up sick off

---

[1] In Carinthia.

the shiny wooden floor. Poor little Rose, she has been almost unbearably stoical, and when a few suppressed tears began to gush silently this evening I was on the point of joining in with a gush of mine. All day I've been bungling everything, translating badly, reading, reading, reading to Rose, feeling heartbreakingly responsible for her, mopping up sick. Janetta is supposed to come home tomorrow – I hope to God she does.

August 2nd

In bed. I've been reading a book about the North face of the Eiger, often in the middle of the night. It's strangely gripping and horrifying, this superhuman and pointless struggle which the climbers keep trying to justify. So is my struggle superhuman and pointless, and all that is at the top of my Eiger (if in the end I devise ways of going from handhold to handhold, tying myself into bivouacs, putting in crampons and pitons) is death. I've been trying to think back to moments of objective pleasure – like the eclipse; to moments when I was able to drag myself along the rope by hauling on my courage – as at Braham. What is so awful here is the sense of disintegration and *dégringolade*, of having no centre or base at all (Ham Spray). This is even symbolized oddly in having left my dear leather writing-case behind – deliberately – for it seemed to hold together the threads of my life. It's *vital* I should set myself to find a new base – it's my only hope, though a slim one.

What does today hold in store? Will Janetta return as she said? How will Rose be? No trouble in the night, thank heaven. On Saturday – that's after three more nights here – I have taken myself a room in the Hotel Alpbacherhof. The Campbell family come here that day, and apart from shortage of rooms there will be more crowd and confusion to which I won't add. Georgia and Julian want to stay as along as possible – I believe others have been asked.

August 3rd

Yesterday morning I telephoned Janetta for instructions about Rose and most of the day the battle to keep anything, even a drop of water inside her, went on. Sent Lisl our maid for the doctor, and his prescription of milkless tea and rusks seemed to work – from then on, 5 p.m., the tide was turned or stemmed.

Janetta did come back, all of them did last night, about ten. The return of humanity at the end of my third day of isolation.

August 6: Alpbacherhof Hotel

The most brilliantly fine day we've had, very hot, and with the mountains so clear against the flawless sky that they seem to bend towards one and be within reach. It's better being here, in a way; I have privacy and peace and no sense of guilt at occupying Janetta's best room. I'm getting on better with Julian, thanks to *him* – he's the one who makes the efforts.

All morning a religious procession shuffled staidly and gloomily round the village. I was interested at first and liked some of the fancy dresses but by no means all. (The older ladies wore small top hats with gold tassels tilted forwards and long black bands down to the ground; some of the young men had guyed their own masculinity by putting on hats with huge feathers and roses. This local silliness is what it's hard to swallow.) Janetta and Julian drove off to Innsbruck to meet the Campbells; meanwhile Georgia and I hung about watching the procession slowly coil and twist round the streets of the town to the accompaniment of muttered prayers, and simple-minded tootling on trumpets and drumbeats. I got increasingly depressed by the stodgy stupidity of it all, the peasant mentality Arthur Koestler seems to admire – which has not the smallest similarity to the wild, obsessional, and exciting drama of popular religious manifestations in Spain. Koestler and Cynthia stood in front as the procession passed – he in his best town suit, head bent, a benign all-embracing, patronizing smile on his face, nodding to the grocer or whoever he knew. On my way to the Alpbacherhof, toiling through the heat before lunch, of course I met him and he pulled up. 'Vell, how did you like it?' 'Very interesting. I am delighted to have seen it,' I said, and asked some questions to give him a chance for one of his favourite lecturettes. 'But I thought it rather sad.' Koestler: 'Oh, no, they are *absolutely* sincere.' F: 'I'm sure of that, but they seem uninspired. However, religion always fills me with gloom.' K: 'Ah, it fills me with *envy*.' F: 'Yes, I suppose it makes them happy. But at that rate one should envy lunatics in their asylum with their delusions.'

All afternoon I sat on my private balcony looking at the best of the view and worked steadily, with a break for a bathe, iced coffee with Julian and Georgia, a visit from Janetta and Robin. Supper at Janetta's house. Seeing the restlessness (not an unhappy one) resulting from seven people living in one large railway carriage, the mingled irritation and pleasure caused by the kittens and their little rolls of shit and big half-eaten mice everywhere, and the impossibility of real privacy, I was glad I had even this rather austere retreat to come to.

August 7th

Very hot yesterday; I plunged into work. Julian came to lunch alone with me, and we had it in the grilling heat of the balcony, ill-protected by an umbrella. Discussion of the effect of Janetta on people – interesting to see it from the viewpoint of the young. He and Georgia are coming out of a period of almost agonizing obsession with her and her values, and it was fascinating for me to open a window and peer back through time into that lost world of desperate fixation, swinging wildly on the swell of favour or disapproval. Having always thought of her as remarkable and adorable, this is nonetheless a new projection of her shadow as dominant, and holding the key to everything in her hands.

August 9th

A glimpse of Alpbach social life: I dined at the Burglerhof with Derek Jackson two nights ago – also Janetta and the children, Julian, Susan. No-one was in sight when I arrived, except a clear-eyed American boy of nineteen who began telling me in one ear about how Derek and Koestler had set on him all afternoon for being an American and believing in American culture. Then Koestler appeared, his face soft like bread soaked in milk, and a very unpleasing monkey-faced Viennese woman was with him. He and Derek, armed neutrals, argued about mathematical problems. I saw Janetta's face crumple and look very brown as she was talking to Koestler. Later she told me he had accused her of being rude to one of his friends, but then he'd grown sentimental and admitted that 'it was love, really', and also that he was rather drunk.

August 13th

This afternoon I at last broached the inviolable mountains, and have come back intoxicated and delighted, with a large bunch of alpine flowers – yellow saxifrage, the wild rhododendron and others I've not yet identified. What a strange thing it is, the challenge of the mountains! All these three weeks I've been looking at their woolly sides askance, hating them, and feeling oppressed and dominated by them. This morning, wintry cold, there were horrible glimpses of snowy summits through the clouds – miniature Eigers hostile to man. When, after solid Sunday lunch the sky began to clear, on the spur of the moment I set up off the most available Wanderweg marked on the map, and picked out with red dots and arrows on walls and trees. Immediate peace, as I very slowly rose, sending the village down a rung or two of the ladder, and reaching up to the snowy heights with each step. That's the great charm: the ever-changing view of things. Great peaks suddenly rise up and peer at one over the shoulders of mild green hills. And then there's something magical about the change of status from fly crawling on the wainscot to eagle up among the clouds. It wasn't much of a climb, but I kept a very slow steady pace. Yesterday's rain had brimmed the streams tearing downhill, and sometimes which was path, which stream, I didn't know. But the banks of flowers led me on as much as the Hansel and Gretel attraction of following the red blobs through woods, across luscious fields and then up the higher reaches of the valley, to the pass I was heading for. I came to a small mountain tarn; pale velvety cows pressed by me, jingling their bells, and driven by a small tow-haired boy. Through the pass and up into the woods, where were masses of shining-leaved bushes of wild rhododendron, and other flowers I'd not yet seen. This was a corniche path slung halfway up the back of the grim peak of the Gratzlspitz. But it was getting late and I turned back, scrambling beside the gushing stream; more flowers, helleborine, a monocotyledon with delicate white flowers balanced on hair-thin stalks. I returned triumphantly sated with these visual and sensual pleasures and pleased to have stretched out and grasped them for myself, and slept like a log for nine long hours.

The grip of the mountains has made itself hard to ignore. Georgia
and Julian aren't tempted by them; Janetta mainly hates, fears and
dreads them; I love and fear them; Susan loves them as a baby
might love a coal fire – not knowing what power they possess, and
bravely (because they give her vertigo). It's always been the same
with me: as soon as I catch sight of them I'm impressed by their
challenge, 'Come and battle with me'. Then if I do tackle them,
the respect and fear are conquered and love gets the upper hand.
Now, with increasing age the desire to stand on their very summits
gives way to the desire to get at and ravish the secret charms of
their higher reaches.

I woke this morning at four after a nightmare – Ralph had died
'again', and I knew that he hadn't been *really* dead before but now
he was; I stood in my bedroom at Ham Spray, half empty of
furniture, feeling a creeping paralysis of loneliness and cold. Woke
to deluging rain and fearful cold which has gone on all day, the
clouds hanging low in the hair of the woods, so low that one can
hardly see the snowy peaks through them, the melancholy sound
(on top of the steady fall of rain) of the spout from the roof
shooting its contents into the valley. Oh, for a fire or radiator! Oh,
what a beastly climate! I'm really glad to be heading home. Yet
here people go about in their cotton dirndls with puff sleeves,
aprons and just an umbrella, and the maids 'dry' the bedding by
shaking it out of the window in the rain.

Janetta has asked me to go back to her house for my last two
nights at Alpbach and I've said I will. She spent the morning
companionably working next to me in the bar. Now the last of
Zoubeida has been packed off to be typed (ten minutes ago) and
I'm theoretically faced with an absence of work. I've not been in
this position since December, and I dread panicking.

How extraordinary that I've said nothing about Berlin! Yet only
four days ago my heart dropped into my boots because of black
headlines three inches high in an indecipherable German newspaper. The Russians had cut off the Western sector completely,
enraged by the increasing flow of refugees from the East. Crisis,
the rattling of sabres, big talk on Janetta's car wireless – 'not only
words' was going to be the answer of the West. Janetta and I
inclined to be despairing – but a wave of common-sense calm from

Robin and Julian (at least able to read the language) restored our equilibrium, probably unjustifiably.

August 24th: London, Hamilton Terrace[1]

I lunched with Burgo two days ago and went with him to a preview of the last film Gary Cooper made before his death. There was a moment when the clutch of Gary and whoever the heroine was, like two monkeys keeping together for warmth, pierced my armour. The shrinkage in my present life comes from the loss of that monkey-warmth; but four days in this racketing Dickensian town haven't quite shattered me yet. It's very nice being alone with Craig in the evenings; such a delightful, kind and understanding companion. Two Spanish servants and a daily keep our bachelor life supported. We sit down to delicious little three-course dinners by candlelight and with half a bottle of claret each evening. Last night we listened to Glück's *Iphigenia* from Edinburgh. And I consulted him about my day's house-hunting, which is what I am here for.

Each day it has rained from a leaden sky and I've rattled round in buses to agents or flats. When I was coming back this afternoon a very old lady appeared on the bus' step: 'Oh, I'm so POOR and ILL! And I've been so worried,' she addressed us all, and willing hands helped her to a seat, encouraged her, told her where she must get off and that the doctor she was going to see was very good. She was reeling into her seat in one direction, while next to me a very old man reeking of drink was falling over backwards in his effort to get off. I couldn't help a stifled snort of laughter and felt I had let down the bus side by such inhumanity. I'm not really discouraged yet in my search, though there seem very few flats going and those very expensive. I may break out, I think, and spend more than Craig thinks I should. I've been able to project myself into two of them, and an unearthly calm prevents my panicking yet – even though the future is so inscrutable.

I've contacted some friends and see there should be no shortage

---

[1] Staying with Craig Macfarlane to look for a flat.

of them here in London. In an odd way I can picture myself here, if only I had a big, light room looking on to trees.

August 28th

I seem to be moving rapidly towards the decision to take a flat in West Halkin Street, Belgravia – that is if it's not already gone. And am amazed that I can look at this constricted possible nest, now hideously furnished with fur rugs and leather chairs, without horror. London, too, seems like a foreign country – yet I think I was right to choose to live here. It's at the opposite pole from Ham Spray, and life in a country cottage would have been a hopelessly pale imitation. I don't think I would have guessed at one result of Ralph's death, which is that I find myself more interested in other people and more able to be at ease with them than I was when the whole body of my libido flowed into the proper channel. It's nine months since Ralph died.

August 31st

The decision to take the West Halkin Street flat is made, the deposit is paid and I'm only terrified lest Craig with his cautious exploration of leases, etc. might let it slip through his fingers, which I would now feel as a serious frustration.

Yesterday Janetta arrived on her dash home from Alpbach and came to see it. She seems to approve greatly and fermented my anxiety to get it. I've been through days when my basic optimism has risen from the marble tomb it has been lying in, days of great heat when London looked exotic and foreign and exciting, so that my antipathy to the idea of living in it suddenly collapsed like a pack of cards; the usual elation too, accompanying a sense of *managing*. I've been absorbed in getting to learn this new town, map in hand, mastering the bus routes and the ways of dealing with special London problems.

Two nights ago Craig and I drove to dinner with the Hills; a luminous evening; we drove through the black quarters of Notting Hill where the houses are painted in tropical colours – yellow, magenta, turquoise blue with grass-green pillars, and everywhere against them the jetty faces above flapping white shirts or crisp pink and green frocks look like holes they are so intensely black,

70

and bodies swing along the pavement as if to inaudible jazz. Nuns on bicycles; Spanish gabbled in every bus. The liveliness of this town I've thought of as moribund, damp and hideous has been a great surprise.

Janetta: It was lovely to see her, something about her well-known personality always has the power to surprise. She was on the verge of tears because thieves had been to Montpelier and taken away the little diamond heart which used to swing so prettily at her wrist – and other things. Last night she came to dinner with me and Craig, very brown in her brown silk frock.

September 2nd: Lambourn

I left London behind yesterday in a state of unimpeached radiance and heat, after a morning spent shopping with Janetta, and lunching off smoked salmon and champagne. She was *piano* with toothache and drugs to ease pain, but everything she does and one can share with her has her own distinct flavour. Arrived here at Gordon House, I went with delight to sit in the coolness of the Gowings' garden. Kees to supper, very nice; the main subject which extended itself at all was concerned with people's attitude to war, and how different was that of a fighting man (Robert) towards the bombing or drowning of enemy babies or sailors to one's own.

This morning my new little car arrived, dumpy, virginal, comic, engaging. I drove it over to Tidcombe to see the Hendersons. I think I shall love it. I do realize how thankful I must be that this new vein of constructiveness has (it does seem) improved my morale out of all recognition, as has the unexpected impression London has made on me.

September 5th

Grey and surly day yesterday, so – there being too little light for Lawrence to paint – he sat in the arbour thinking about his painting. As he sat looking into the woods with his easel in front of him he discovered that what he saw, with the closer edge of his visual field and the greatest depth in the middle, was much like the hollow half of a sphere. He sat as it were inside a globe, and as he's at present trying to think of the world in abstract terms he became preoccupied all day by trying to work out how various mathematical shapes could be fitted into this hemisphere. (Hexagons for instance, composed as they were of six isosceles triangles.) Seized with the desire to demonstrate it practically, he rushed to the village toy shop and bought a large child's ball *on approval* (I saw it in the hall in a plastic bag, as large as a melon), then sat trying to fit hexagons onto its surface with a ballpoint pen. *They wouldn't go.* This great discovery delighted him, tho' I can't remember what he deduced from it. But it delights me too as being so characteristic of his original and eccentric nature. Then he had a job to rub off the ink marks, but finally it was done, the ball returned to the shop and at dinner he told us how he had spent the afternoon, Julia staring at him as if she'd never seen him before in her life.

September 6th

Much talk with the Gowings about decorating my new flat – both helpful in their different ways. Julia is of course perfectionist to an impracticable degree. She says, 'If a wall has to be a setting for pictures it must be considered in relation to *each* of those pictures.' F: 'But the walls must be painted before the pictures come out of store.' J: 'Oh, that's *very* serious.' (Looking horrorstruck) 'Couldn't you have them taken out and sent up first?' I am enjoying turning round colour combinations in my head, and at times I feel a rising excitement and even confidence as when I am just going to arrange flowers in a vase.

September 8th: Long Crichel House

On I move once more to shelter again under the kind wing of friends – Eardley[1] and Raymond at Crichel. I buzzed there in stately fashion in the little white egg of my car. It's very, very nice to be here. I do think I've made headway since the last time with its crushing moment of panic, grief and lostness. I am a bit more stabilized now. Relaxed, communicative evening last night talking to Raymond and Eardley and listening to Haydn quartets. Raymond greeted me most warmly, started 'You look . . .' and then, seeing there was nothing to be said about my looks, fell silent!

[1] Knollys.

This sort of tiny incident delights me. I know I look appalling, worn and hagridden and even older than I am, though Julia was kind enough to say she'd noticed a change for the better. Why then find it delightful? Just because actions, tones of voices and expressions have proved again that they are an easy language to read, which can be deciphered in a flash.

September 10th

Duncan[1] came the night before last. I can't help wondering what the inner equation is by which he deals with a situation more or less like mine[2] – the withdrawal of half the interest, vital flow of his life – and realizing that as little as he betrays it, so probably do I. In his stained ill-fitting suit he looks rather like a Jewish pawnbroker, standing a little apologetically and as if about to shuffle off or rub his hands together; rather hunched, looking up and blinking anxiously at us from his still forget-me-not-blue eyes in a crumpled rose-petal face. Yet his air of apology, seeming to say, 'I don't really know how to behave. I'm not concerned with the world and its values'. This childlike innocence wouldn't take in anyone, nor does it take in Duncan himself. He has an excellent opinion of himself and quite right too, is probably well aware of his terrific power to charm, and certainly confident that his values are the right ones, and that what he excludes and doesn't know about isn't worth knowing. I think this self-confidence and lack of self-criticism (which could also be called unselfconsciousness) is the salient thing about his character, and derives from the fact that so many people have loved him and been in love with him, and Bloomsbury always spoiled him and laughed delightedly at his half-unconscious wit. Buoyed up by which, he's been able to dedicate himself simply and directly to what he wanted to do. He must be ranked, along with Bunny, among the happiest men alive.

I'd been saying to Eardley on a walk that I wished one could talk to him directly about his grand-daughters, or Angelica[3] as his daughter. Eardley thought it impossible. We wondered if Vanessa's death might make a difference. And then David Cecil came to

[1] Grant.
[2] Vanessa's death.
[3] Garnett.

dinner and did it – referred quite gaily and unconsciously to 'your grand-daughter'. No sign of surprise from Duncan, yet I can't help feeling it *was* a slight shock to him because he *had* overlooked the fact that everyone in the world knows.

September 12th

Each time I come here I feel more contented and at my ease with my male friends and their male preoccupations. One evening Raymond, Eardley and I got talking about women's rivalry with each other – they both agreed that it was dangerous to introduce two female friends, as they would compete for male attention! I could make little impression on this curiously naive cracker-motto philosophy. They illustrated it by an awful weekend when Hester[1] and Elizabeth Bowen were invited together. Women, they said (kindly exempting me and Cressida[2]) couldn't argue except aggressively and emotionally; women dislike finding too many other women in any gathering and like being the only one. I suggested that they were thinking of men (and indeed, women also) as a single sex, regardless of whether they were homo- or heterosexual, whereas two homos of either sex could be drawn together by mutual attraction. There was a silence and I felt I'd broken an unwritten law, but later on Raymond returned to this idea as if it struck him there might be something in it.

September 17th

Just as I was consoling myself that I was beginning to come to terms with my existence, yesterday's change of scene brought a pitiful sag and wavering. As when trying to go through a hoop in croquet, very much depends on keeping confidence flying, mainly it would seem by auto-suggestion. Courage, courage . . . You *can* do it all right if you try. Leaving Crichel was like going back to school, and yesterday had the blank, washed-out quality, neither here nor there, of the last day of the holidays.

Then came a flood of longing for the only companion whose company was also relaxation. Now I can only relax in solitude, and to do that I risk futile restlessness.

---

[1] Chapman, writer.
[2] Ridley, née Bonham-Carter.

Last night I felt that coming to Cranborne again was somehow an ordeal requiring a superhuman effort. A walk with Rachel, through green tunnels of trees. Her maturity coloured by confidence is like the ripeness of a fruit that has steadily grown against a wall of security in the warm sun of family affection. All of them are talkers – Jonathan perhaps talks most. Hugh has more reserves, is often thoughtful and content to be silent. They all break happily into imitations and observations on what's going on, and (most important) pounce on general ideas. David declares he gets over-agitated in argument and regrets it afterwards, and described himself and Iris Murdoch shouting at each other and jumping up and down on the carpet during a disagreement.

September 18th: Stokke

Moved on here yesterday, driving Mini with more confidence through blazing heat. Stokke always reminds me painfully of Ham Spray. I walked with Mary over her fields, and helped her weed a bed.

I've not said that while I was at the Cecils' the chief Nuclear Disarmament supporters, including eighty-nine-year-old Bertie Russell, were put in jail because they refused to be bound over not to meet and 'sit down' in Trafalgar Square on Battle of Britain day, which was several days ago. In spite of this, hundreds did meet and sit down, and one and all who were still there at midnight were taken to jail, including Nicky, Harriet Hill and Henrietta Garnett. Slowly, painfully but eagerly they described their grim experience to an audience of Janetta, Anne Hill and me. Harriet was rather tragic about it, Nicky came out at her best. I got her to tell me about it all in more detail yesterday – how rough the police had been, hauling them along the ground by their arms, throwing a young man on top of them when they lay there; how an inspector had kicked her; how the police had called them 'stupid cows' and asked each other, 'What shall we do? Shit on them?' About their bewilderment and uncertainty and the grimness then and flatness now; how it had been almost a relief to get in the Black Maria, but the journey rattling along in cells had horrified them; how no-one gave them anything to eat until they were brought up at Clerkenwell Court and fined £1 each at lunch-time next day; how they were crowded into an airless cell with a lavatory in it which everyone had to use; how some were wet and shivering from being thrown into the fountains; how sixty of them slept on a huge 'mattress' or 'sheet' but the police woke them up by raking the different wireless stations every hour like the Gestapo; how Nicky had testified to her beliefs when asked if she had anything to say; how anxious she felt now about what had happened to her friends, and whether she had done what she should.

This situation has aroused indignation even among some Conservatives and started lots of arguments, whereas among my friends were some who spoke intolerantly about them all '*wanting* to be roughly handled, longing for it'. In the afternoon I ventured to set my own position to Nicky: 'Why don't you "sit down" since you're a pacifist and against the bomb?' she asked me. 'We need some grey heads.' I said because I didn't think 'sitting down' convinced anyone, only arguments could do that. (*She* wouldn't be convinced that the bomb was right just because people who believed it was 'sat down'), that I wasn't, however, against any form of demonstration so long as they didn't adopt the very means they were against – some form of violence, and that blocking roads or railways was that. Useless to say: 'Yes, but the alternative is so much worse – the bomb.' That was the warmongers' own argument. She got excited momentarily, but then was prepared to consider my points; there's no doubt she feels violently about it – and Lord knows she's entitled to, young as she is and enjoying her life and wanting to go on doing so.

September 22nd: Montpelier Square

I hesitated whether or not to go with Janetta to an evening reunion with Joan Rayner's[1] group of intellectuals – Cyril, Quennell, Bowra, and so on. Decided my vitality wasn't equal to it, and I'm glad I did, for the description given by Magouche and Janetta next morning was uninviting. Cyril had snubbed Janetta. Social life here in London, rolling, clattering and thundering all day long, is a very different affair from the country variety: and there is so much to stimulate conversation that it's less of an effort. I'm not sure if less thought goes to make it, or whether the swift onrush of more and more talk effaces what has gone before even more completely. I

[1] Now Leigh-Fermor.

cannot help probing my wounds and speculating as to what effect being unable to communicate with an alter ego has on my mental process – do I now cease to have those thoughts I used to love to exchange with Ralph?

Lunch with Bunny yesterday. He has thought of a solution of the Berlin crisis and wants to present it to some high-placed official or other. Talked sympathetically of the young people and their anti-bomb protests, also of Angelica's bastardy. He showed that he was unaware that it was universally known, and said that they had not told his four daughters but realized that Amaryllis[1] had somehow heard, 'told by her school friends'. The reason he gave for discretion was consideration for Clive's feelings.

October 2nd

Shuttled back to Montpelier after another venture into the country – Hilton Hall[2] this time, ramshackle, bohemian, improvised, beautiful house full of beautiful things neglected, tattered and thick with cobwebs. Music in confusion and disarray, rolls of dust under the bed, bathroom like a junk-shop, the basin leaning out of the wall, furniture propped on books, stains, cracks everywhere, no bulbs in the lights, a smeared single coat of paint on the walls of my room, not enough blankets on the bed. But delicious meals, plenty to drink, and every object chosen with taste. I do react somewhat against the do-it-yourself philosophy, by which everything home-made is by definition held to be better than everything that's not – for that simply isn't so. But it is a very warm, lively civilization, lit up by the presence of Bunny and Angelica's four blooming daughters. Two were making their first ventures away from home – Amaryllis came down on Saturday after her first days in a theatrical school, displaying a budding actressy manner under which one can read intelligence, sweetness and enthusiasm for life. Poor Henrietta, the most dazzlingly attractive of the four and the most interesting, is being sacrificed (so it seems to me) to some strange principle, by having to spend a term in a frightful Do-the-boys-Hall of a coaching establishment, with a régime of old-fashioned austerity. She came to lunch on Sunday, and was funny

---

[1] The eldest of Bunny and Angelica's four daughters. She became an actress.
[2] With the Garnett family.

about the bleakness, stinginess and horrible food, and about being turned out-of-doors to walk for two hours in the rain in the flat East Anglian landscape. I felt indignant that she should be subjected to this and perhaps for ever associate work and learning with everything repressive and uncivilized.

With Bunny I had many conversations on all topics, and discussions of the new volume of his memoirs he's writing – very mixed, a curious mawkishness comes in occasionally while other very tricky situations like Ray's illness and death brought tears to his eyes.[1] Angelica has thrown up her violin and hardly ever plays the piano, but spends every odd moment thrumming very old, pure music on a guitar; and when she sits with her family in the evening talking isn't enough; she feverishly knits. I wondered about the effect of Vanessa's death in bringing her closer to Duncan.

My flat is now *really mine*. Today I received the keys, ordered a fireplace and arranged about the electricity.

October 3rd

Janetta had friends in yesterday evening. Talked of suicide with her and Raymond, who held it was always an insane action. In this as in other things he said I found him very different from his country self: a stay with millionaires in Venice had brought out all that is most un-serious and worldly in him. We talked of 'human butterflies': again Raymond defended them but no-one could think of any except Raymond himself, and an Italian lady he had recently met. Paddy Leigh-Fermor bounced round the room thundering: 'But they're appalling! The Italian upper classes are FRIGHTFUL! – weak, philistine, *vain, DULL!*' Next it was whether we were being fogies or not in failing to appreciate modern painting and drama. Was this a period of decline? Raymond and Paddy thought so – Patrick Kinross said every fogy had said this of every period of civilization. I said it worried me to miss so much possible pleasure and to think we might be like the people who cackled with laughter at the Impressionists. Janetta said in her gentlest voice that it didn't worry her *at all* – there were so many other things she greatly enjoyed. The clock ticked on to one, and the mixture of personalities in the room was violently stirred, bubbling

---

[1] His first wife, my sister.

and subsiding by turns. This whirling restlessness and public expense of spirit is perhaps typical of London life, and I don't altogether care for it. Upstairs, gratefully snatching at oblivion. London is an iron lung, which grips one and forces one to go through the motions of a living being almost against one's will. I shall miss Janetta terribly when she goes abroad in two days' time. Her kindness and generosity have been deeply touching to me; I think or hope I've managed to fit in with her way of life (not-planning ahead) and it will be an effort to wean myself so as to carry on my life here without her. My flat is now infested with decorators and I 'hope' to move into it at the end of the month. I long above all for some regular work.

A visit with Little Barbara to Saxon[1] in hospital made me really admire her. She was so long-suffering and truly kind, and her kindness was so effective in giving Saxon happiness, that I feel her to contain real goodness, and regret the critical things I sometimes say about her. But oh, the sadness of seeing this poor old man, all dignity gone but his delicate ivory beauty remaining, with his paralysed arm folded on his breast like the broken wing of a bird, his mumbling words, his abandoned coughs and sighs, and the look of sensitive intelligence coming from his bright eyes. Then I began to understand that he wasn't really unhappy, because for long years he has wanted but little here below and that mostly attention; and he gets that from the pretty little Malay nurses who peer into his white face with their velvet eyes. But I felt thankful that Ralph never had to put up with that sort of conclusion to his life, and remained so entirely himself to his last day. I came away from Dollis Hill with renewed respect for Barbara and a conviction that euthanasia should be legalized.

Old Bloomsbury – what's left of it – and its hangers-on were at a private view of Vanessa's paintings – Duncan, Roy Harrod, Bunny, Quentin, Angus Davidson, Le Bas, Michael MacCarthy.

October 14th: Knapp House, Iping

I dived (yesterday afternoon) into the clashing roaring stream plunging south-west out of London. How have softly vulnerable

---

[1] Sydney-Turner, mystery man of Bloomsbury, who had loved Barbara all his adult life.

shell-less humans managed to adapt themselves to this cataclysmic and continuous racket? Felt that I was involved in a compulsive rat-race, while being nothing at all like a rat. Then suddenly it was the loveliest possible autumn day as I whirled through Surrey and found myself all at once among my childhood haunts, looking at the Devil's Punch Bowl, unchanged and smiling in the afternoon sun, its trees turning gold. At Hindhead I parked my Mini and wandered out to look. But it wasn't so much the sights that carried me nostalgically backward as the smell, which I seemed never to have smelt between the ages of twelve and sixty – inconceivably fresh, warm, sweet and aromatic, made up of bracken, moss, heather I suppose, earth and rotting tangles of roots, but contriving also to suggest the fur coat and kid gloves of M.A.M.[1] going out to a party – Mother Earth, perhaps?

October 24th: Montpelier Square

Janetta comes back in two days' time. I look forward to seeing her. Rose still in bed with a temperature. The last decisions about my flat have been made with a delightful Mr Bielinski, whose most critical comment is, 'I think that would look rather *seelly*.'

Pleasant dinner with the Campbells. An apologetic seal-like female dog lay on the sofa; it was the unforgettable pet of Craigie Aitchison, Susan's painter friend, who came in himself just before we left, with his large egg-shaped head wobbling gently from side to side, talking and laughing quietly, more to himself than the rest of the company, which included Julian Jebb. I was very pleased to see him again and drove him back in Mini.

I went this evening to a Wigmore Hall concert by a Polish pianist, a pupil of Casals and recommended by James Strachey. He played four Mozart sonatas and never once made one regret how he was playing them. James was in the second row, and I moved up beside him in the interval, where I had a better view of the magical hands and the intent, humorous guinea-pig face seeming to hunt down the musical phrase with wide-open, seeking eyes. The solvent of the music made me conscious of my deep affection for James – that lovable man.

I looked in afterwards at a nearby café for some food, and soon

---

[1] My mother.

in came the Polish demi-god, transformed into a tiny little harassed man in a rather shiny suit and sat eating a plateful of bad cheap food and drinking beer.

November 11th: West Halkin Street

Here I am alone, on my desert island, amazed to realize that I've been here and slept here in my solitude for over a week. Each night I hear thumping footsteps and platitudinous voices overhead and in an odd way I find them comforting. Now, a Saturday, I'm testing myself out by staying in London for the weekend, and it pours with rain from a grey sky. Yesterday for the first time my flat seemed to come alive and now I look round at what I've planned and constructed and wonder what it's really like. The hall with its rich, dark Indian pattern wallpaper is still heaped with books and without a rug. The bedroom, soft peaceful grey and white, bow-window, countrified pictures (landscapes, cats, owls), and the sitting-room warm pink, mustard, green and purple, have emerged just as I meant, and now the books, china and piano complete it. I asked Eardley what sort of a room it seemed. 'Very scholarly,' he replied.

November 12th

There was a special meeting of the Memoir Club at Charleston last weekend, gathered to hear Roy Harrod read aloud fifty-year-old letters between Lytton and Maynard. It was a fascinating correspondence, strikingly modern in language; communicating closest friendship and a desire to share feelings and thoughts, but with values in some respects different from those of today. Love seemed less exclusively a matter of sex. Though tossed by jealousy, despair, hope and ecstasy, it was total love; what's more, for intellectual equals instead of bell-hops and sailors. Lytton at first confided his love for Duncan. Maynard was full of sympathy, declared himself 'in love with the fact of Lytton and Duncan's mutual love'. The drama came to a crisis when Duncan suddenly began an affair with Maynard himself, and Lytton was told and wrote a touching, rather noble letter about it. But his friendship for Maynard never really recovered. Lytton's earlier letters were brilliantly good and I thought perhaps this blow had produced the sense of emotional mummification he developed later.

Before the reading began, Duncan had met me in the darkness at Lewes station and while driving me erratically to Charleston explained that Roy was anxious lest he should find these letters embarrassing. 'I suppose I ought to, but I don't, and I'm only worried whether other people may be embarrassed on my account.' I found Clive looking older and rather thin. Roy arrived after dinner, spry, confident and talkative. The extraordinary house, so lovingly decorated with paint everywhere, was ice-cold and uncomfortable but provided us with good food, abundant wine and lively talk. The potent Bloomsbury atmosphere encircled us. I was given Vanessa's bedroom, looking out on the frozen garden trimmed with a neat edging of grey shrubs; there was a bath behind a screen in one corner and faceless portraits on the walls. The reading went on nearly all Saturday and Sunday in the studio, Roy reading well but very fast while we sat round in a circle now augmented by Sebastian,[1] Angus[2] and Leonard.[3] Between lunch and tea some of us put on coats and walked on the slopes of the downs. Leonard, now eighty, with his noble face hanging in string-like folds, walked up the steep hill with me, easily outpacing Angus.

November 15th

I hate doing my life sentence and would gladly abandon it for ever – would like to lay down my life as one drops a handkerchief. Death is always in my thoughts now, and tears make a high-water mark in the inside of my head. Why live unloved, unwarmed (who cares if I do or not?) with no-one to laugh with and share my preoccupations? Why haul and heave to pull my courage up from the bottom of the well it has dropped into? Since one must fix on some landmark ahead, I'm going to try to think of going to Spain in just over a month's time, as a prisoner thinks of the next visit he's allowed. Misery is a dreadful acid which dissolves the mental processes, obliterates the memory and slows up the responses – an attempt to commit suicide on the part of the brain.

[1]   W.H.J. Sprott, professor of philosophy.
[2]   Davidson, translator from Italian.
[3]   Woolf.

November 16th

I have been navigating a bad patch of my London life, and yesterday was one of my worst days. I couldn't stop crying and my skeleton life stood naked with bare bones projecting before my eyes. My lack of interest in living made dozens of trifling things go wrong. With relief I sank into bed, to be woken by a wrong number at four. Talking just now to Janetta on the telephone I was so aware of the dire acuteness of my crisis that I felt surprised it didn't communicate itself to her. But after almost a year of bereavement, in which everyone has been infinitely kind and I have probably seemed to be well on the way to recovery, how can anyone possibly realize that it's *worse* now than ever, or if they do, how can they fail to be bored by the fact? *Better*, a little, today. The sun shines. I realize why this access of despair has come: all this last year I have been preparing to live my new life, by demolishing the old. Now I've got to begin doing it and it's a ghastly mockery and I hate it.

Better. Why? Janetta turned up to lunch, as did Julia; and it seems she too had touched rock bottom yesterday. Meanwhile the dread animal that lies within turned over in his basket, and somehow I feel more able now to go on, for a few more steps, anyway.

November 20th

I'm back in my flat after a weekend at Stokke, with Mary and John Julius Norwich. He's a nice, clever, interested young man, apparently almost aggressively normal and well-adjusted. I walked out, each of the two cold autumn days, under hedges of faded papery leaves, drained of all colour. Then turning past the foresters' cottages quietly smoking into the still air I began to climb the path which leads back to Stokke. It seemed to me I saw someone standing at the top near the gate and for a moment I vividly, passionately imagined it was my darling Ralph, standing there with his loving welcoming face, and my longing for him was something concrete and solid hanging in the chilly air.

I have begun on work in the shape of trying to edit Desmond MacCarthy's letters, at the request of his family. I have begun to return hospitality: Cochemés, Lawrence, Japps[1] have all been here. Discussing suicide with the Cochemés, Joan looked at me with her round eyes and said: 'We're all afraid of *you* committing suicide.' Life and death seem at times so triflingly different from each other (a squiggle here, a line there), that it doesn't seem odd at all to talk lightly of suicide. But I've done nearly a year of my life-sentence and where have I got to?

November 28th

To Lawford[2] last weekend: when I entered the silent dark hall of the beautiful but melancholy house there was no-one to be seen; then a door opened and Phyllis appeared, hauling on the collar of a barking, straining animal. From then on this creature took to itself the star part. It was a large handsome pointer with a satiny loose-fitting coat of blue-black and whitest white: the black in the three large blobs with other small dots peppered around it. Lithe and strong, it bounded about with uncontrollable vitality or slumped down on the rug and gazed out of bloodshot eyes. Rocco is the centre of Phyllis' world; she talks to him in a quiet, low reasonable tone, entirely without effect, and he goes on devouring shoes, hats and corks. None of us was allowed for one second to forget him, and it was lucky that he had an endearing personality since we had to focus on it all the time.

A lovely, still, cold weekend, with the salt-marsh and river lying pale beneath the garden. Comfort, relaxation with company. An afternoon excursion wooding with Phil in the Land Rover, bumping along under the oak avenue, dusk falling and a light drizzle. A visit from Randolph Churchill. Heavens, how boring is time spent with someone drunk from the start and refusing to let anyone speak. For four mortal hours we endured his insistent personality. The dog was less tolerant; he broke out barking and had to be taken out of the room. I admired the way Phil and Phyllis handled Randolph, expecially when Phil offered to drive his guest home, and Randolph replied, 'Where I dines I sleep.'

---

[1] Darsie, painter, and Lucila, his Spanish wife.
[2] The Nicholses in Essex.

December 1st

Yesterday's anniversary is over. I thought I was immune to such considerations, but realized I didn't want to be alone in the evening and was glad to go with Isobel to the film of *The Turn of the Screw*. A year of my sentence is *done*: impossible thought. I have had a nice musical evening with Ralph Jarvis and Laurie Lee, been anxiously stirred and touched by Burgo in his new flat, and gone to a private view of Henry Lamb's pictures (where Pansy did the honours). And so on, so on, so on. I work intermittently at Desmond's letters, changing my view every few moments as to how good they are.

December 2nd: Chatsworth

I embarked for Chatsworth yesterday afternoon with Janetta, Andrew Devonshire, Adrian Daintrey[1] and Patrick Kinross.[2] It was already dark and wet when Janetta called for me in a comfortable limousine and we sped across London to St Pancras. Beneath the great straddling station arch were trucks and trucks of Christmas parcels and a large, patient crowd. Among men with guitars and coated greyhounds we found our party. The loud-speaker repeatedly announced delays to our train and we relapsed into our First Class carriage an hour late. Standing in the train bar drinking whiskey, Adrian Daintrey, a delightful and amusing character, told me at length and in detail about Edna, a prostitute with whom he has had some sort of relationship for the last ten years. How I envy such communicativeness! As if in a dream I abandoned myself to the journey, including the silken smoothness of our drive through the darkness to the great house, waiting for us floodlit. Beautiful, sumptuous, splendid objects loomed up, and – still in a dream – I walked into my palatial bedroom lined and curtained with dark red velvet, with its fine gilt and white four-poster, and a quiet maid waiting.

Now it's morning and I lie in bed, a huge breakfast greedily eaten, looking at the exquisite proportion of pale blue sky to pale green landscape seen through the enormous windows. I slept badly and feel hardly equal to facing the day. To do so, I try forcibly to

[1] Painter.
[2] Writer.

turn my thoughts outwards. Daintrey, for instance. Is he lonely? I like him.

December 3rd

Dazzled by the great beauty of this place (the park, waterfalls, fountains, statues and marvellous contents of the house – Rembrandts, Tintorettos), draught upon draught of it. In cold bright sun we walked across the vast sheet of greensward, past the tall plume of the fountain blowing sideways, to see some remarkable crocuses flowering out of doors; through the orchid houses, and rows of cyclamens in pots.

This beautiful house, and it really *is* beautiful in an unforgettable way, nonetheless is a *thing*, a great *object* reared up indestructibly in the middle of vulnerable human relationships. What can anyone do against it? It is the master, the strongest force. I'm constantly reminded of Henry James: it is what might happen in one of his plots (perhaps does) that a house should be the most important character, just as the dog was at Lawford. Snow began to fall quietly outside, lying like a cloth on the stone table on the terrace, and the sky grew dark. Andrew took us to see more and more remote treasures – gold and silver stood gleaming in glass-fronted cupboards, looking far more alive than the small man whose whole life consisted in polishing and handling it. Much longer here and one would be defeated and routed by this formidable house and its cargo of rare objects. Adrian and I spent several hours turning over marvellously lovely drawings by Rembrandt or Inigo Jones. He manages to keep his original and comic personality intact; for my part I grew steadily more consciously expressionless.

When I reached home at tea-time, I found a letter from Eardley saying he proposed we set forth to drive to Spain in little more than a fortnight, and also a touching one from Gerald, written on November 30th: 'This is the saddest of anniversaries and I thought I'd just write you a letter to say – but what is there to say? Only that I haven't forgotten it.'

December 5th

I spend a lot of my time in uncontrollable tears. How can I get a grip on myself?

December 7th

Why, WHY did I ever struggle on? Was it some faint stirring of the life-instinct, lack of courage – or even the reverse, a perverted desire to be brave? I have spent now two days in *passionately* longing to be dead – floundering through the barest necessities of life. Janetta and I lunched with Boris yesterday, after clambering the dusty ladders to admire his mosaics in the Roman Catholic Cathedral. As we praised them, he laughed softly. Afterwards I went with Janetta to buy Christmas toys at the Army and Navy Stores, and watched her stroking teddy bears while the tears rolled uncontrollably down my face. Poor Janetta – I felt appalled to rest weight on her already overburdened and fragile boat.

December 14th

Better again, and resolving, for a while at least, not to harp so much on my own misery.

Dinner with the Kees last night, to meet the present literary editor of the *New Statesman*, Karl Miller, and his very pregnant, jolly wife. Arrived at eight-thirty to find the wife waiting (as I was) for the others who returned from a cocktail party, wound-up, with their wheels still whirring. Karl Miller is an intelligent auto-intoxicated, young and ambitious Scot; doesn't want to hear anything from anyone else, but just to do his own turn ad lib, which happens to be skilful and often funny. But few people want to spend the whole evening laughing heartily at someone else's capers; it was like a night out with stockbrokers. There was quickfire, showing-off talk about the situation in the Congo, which I can't understand anyway; also some sex-badinage. I liked Terry Kilmartin, literary editor of the *Observer*, but I didn't enjoy the evening much, especially when Robert said to me: 'How are you getting along? Are you enjoying London? Cynthia thinks you really *love* the rat-race!' I tried to put my mood of rejecting life into a semi-comical frame, but Robert wouldn't have it and swept it aside – 'Oh no, I'm *sure* you're enjoying yourself.' What can he possibly have meant?

December 21st

Eardley and I set off for Spain two days ago and they have gone well, in marvellous weather, crisp and cloudless, frosty, with a clear pale blue sky. I think we shall manage very well together; we've got on to a plane of easy talk. Our first night was spent at Granville, the Normandy *plage* Ralph and I visited a few years ago and vowed to come back to. Yesterday to Madame de Sevigné's Les Rochers; I was moved to see the allées – 'les charmes' – she planted, and imagined her showing them to her son. They are small and stunted still.

December 24th

Lying on my cell bed at Palencia. Eardley and I are getting along very well. No *gêne*, and I think no irritation.

There is so much to talk about – after five days we have not run out, nor been reduced to compulsively observing our fellow-guests. And the constant movement, the steady stream of visual and other impressions has worked well. Bordeaux is quite spoilt – the Chapon Fin modernized and its restaurant temporarily shut; the lovely old market being pulled down; tiny new trees in the allées. 'I expect they'll have cut down the quincunxes,' said Eardley, and they practically had. In Spain the best has been a nice old-fashioned hotel full of clocks at San Sebastian and that glorious town Salamanca where we lunched today. After still, sunny and frosty weather across France, Spain has lashed us with rain and cold winds, indigo clouds scudding over the plateau of Castile and a strange apricot light on the horizon.

December 29th: Churriana[1]

Journey's end, and I sit up in bed in my long cold room at Churriana. Am I going to be able to stand the discomforts (but if they – the Brenans – do, why can't I?): the lack not only of bath but any hot water *at all*, save what is boiled up in kettles; the plugless lavatory, smelly and dripped-over, the *cold*, compared to my warm London flat? Yet everything is beautiful and spacious, and I'm

[1] The Brenans' village.

ashamed to be so materialistic. But I'm going to master the technique of living here I *think*, that's to say enjoy the immense bounties offered me by the Brenans and avoid Julia-esque carping at the discomforts. Against the latter I put up small stubborn rearguard actions. I've been given a tiny electric kettle in my bedroom and this I plug in at night for my hotwater-bottle and at mornings for an all-over wash – about a pint of boiling water does it, and I feel it would be death to give it up and lapse into squalor. The smell in the lavatory I combat by flinging the window wide open when I go there. The outside air today is sweet and warm, but I don't think anyone notices, any more than they do the smell. At the top of the house, a sort of roof room, formerly open on all sides, is now glassed-in, and here I have my work table. It is perfectly beautiful, each window framing a different view, Malaga on one side, the nearer mountains on another, tall bamboos and the garden on the third and fourth. The sun pours in on me now and I feel fortunate to be here and allowed to exist in this sweet peace. A soft sound of gobbling turkeys comes up from below. Gerald has given me his autobiography to read.

1962

January 1st: Churriana

As I approached the end of Gerald's autobiography[1] (about the War) I found myself recoiling from going on – not that it wasn't interesting. But because his picture of Ralph in the War, accurate as far as it goes I dare say, but infused with all his own (Gerald's) feelings of envy, hero-worship and mockery mixed, is in any case not 'my' Ralph, I realized from Gerald's letters some time ago that he felt a deep subconscious need to discharge on me everything he had felt and thought about Ralph all his life long. Last night, since I'd reached that part of his book, he began to do so; a torrent of words, and of thoughts and impressions tumbled from his mouth, many of which I didn't want to hear; they fell like heavy stones on a raw bleeding wound. Gerald is an extraordinary man. He responds in such an original way to books and the visual world, and yet is blind as a bat to other people's feelings. Or am I being impossibly fastidious? It was in fact extremely painful to me to sit in the battering fusillade of his impression of Ralph, as he talked on and on egotistically, with glazed eyes, *relieving* himself as it were, and the effort to respond with temperate, balanced remarks exhausted me. There was much, too, about Carrington, justifying himself as he always does. 'Nothing had happened,' he said when Valentine's disclosures made Ralph so furiously jealous. Except, as it turned out, that Gerald and Carrington had fallen violently in love and had been secretly meeting and kissing! Because he had 'no thought of going further', Gerald exonerates himself utterly, and thinks Ralph unreasonable to have minded the treachery and deception as he did. I dread having more of these long-dormant

[1] *A Life of One's Own* was published later in 1962.

bombs exploded round me. I work at Desmond's letters nearly all the mornings in the roof room.

Gamel and Gerald seem unusually happy together, strange pair that they are. Gamel has modified her acerbity to him, but does almost nothing all day but read science fiction. The more the servants are paid the less they do and the more Gerald and Gamel feel they must clear away plates and fetch the innumerable things they forget. We are always running out of salt or marmalade and Rosario[1] goes about with a deeply worried expression.

January 4th

Went by bus to Marbella yesterday because Hetty and Jason[2] were due to arrive and I thought a few hippies might tag along too.

Got back to find Hetty installed. She appalled me at first with her vulgarity and crudeness, her silly and loud social manner, but in the course of the evening I came to recognize her genuine friendliness and warm-heartedness, though such a simply euphoric attitude to life could never be sympathetic to me. I even grew to be able to look at her oblong suet-coloured face and the unbrushed red-dyed hair that hangs round it, without aversion. Little Jason has just been up into my work sanctum and I only narrowly succeeded in preventing him dropping one of the cats out of a window.

January 9th

Our life here is one of cold grey austerity with little or no sensual pleasure, and the sun after two brief peeps at us, has disappeared again. This morning at breakfast, I had a discussion with Gerald about asceticism. It's a surprise to me to find how deeply ingrained in him it is, deriving he says from reading at school that Hannibal's army was defeated by giving way to luxury! At times I feel nipped and deadened by this bleakness; by the dust and dirt everywhere

---

[1] Gerald's housekeeper.
[2] Gerald's latest hippy girl-friend and her little boy. A number of hippies had drifted to southern Spain. Besides giving shelter to Hetty and her little boy, Gerald had rather comically adopted some of their manners and language himself.

– the fluff lying inches deep all over my bedroom floor, mixed with feathers and bits of paper; by the total disregard of comfort; the cold, kept at bay with such a constant struggle; the war against the cats, messing in the passages and rooms (the passage stinks of them), licking the butter and being sick on the beds; ('they can't help it,' Gamel murmurs fondly); by the smelly unwashed lavatory; by the unloved, uncared-for meals (baked apples twice a day every day, and uneatably tough steak); by the fact that it's been impossible to get any clothes washed since I arrived except what I can do myself in my borrowed baths. Yet all this seems shamefully base ingratitude. Mary Campbell has arrived at the Cónsula and my heart leaps up at the thought of seeing her today and being warmed by her sunlike radiance.

There have been plenty of social contacts. Eardley, Duncan and the Creightons[1] drove over from San Roque, luckily striking a fine day. I was glad to be able to be hospitable and to feel they had enjoyed themselves as I knew they did: drinks here, lunch in the sun out of doors at Antonio Martin's, sight-seeing and shopping in Malaga, lit by rosy afternoon sun and under a bright blue sky. As darkness fell I was in a pottery shop where I'd taken Duncan to buy Nijar bowls; suddenly the streets were full of a dense, excited crowd. We parted, Duncan to the Hotel Cataluña, I to get a bus or taxi home – but I was caught, hemmed-in and trapped by the procession of decorated floats for the Reyes Magos celebrations and the screaming crowds lining the Alameda and the Calle de Larios. Seeking a taxi vainly, running hither and thither, asking policemen, being told to wait on a corner for a 'momentito' and being left there for good, I nearly panicked, but luckily I found a café, ordered a large whiskey, and sat there drinking it until the procession had filed by, Father Christmases, camels, elephants and snowmountains.

January 19th

Gerald, Gamel and I walked to Torremolinos yesterday afternoon, Gerald springing along in front (his head set woodenly looking neither right nor left, with the expression of a bulldog on a trail, his eyes unseeing except for a sudden dart towards some wayside

---

[1]   Basil and Frances, a highly civilized elderly couple.

plant); Gamel creeping behind; I uneasily shifting from one to the other. We talked of what we thought about when alone, and whether we were most preoccupied with present, past or future. Gerald declared he 'never thought about the past'. Gamel countered quite crossly that she'd never known anyone who talked so endlessly about their schooldays and childhood. She liked thinking about her earlier life, not recent years because they were too dull – nothing had happened. She also said revealingly that when she thought of the past in terms of visual imagery *she saw herself* among the other figures.

Back to a quiet evening. Gerald and Gamel both snored in armchairs round the fire while I read about the stars. Hetty's little boy Jason is with us during her absence in Morocco and comes for reassurance, poor worried little creature, that he is really the centre of the universe.

January 21st

As Gerald and I went into Malaga yesterday afternoon he monologuized all the way down the road to the bus, and continued as we wandered round the town on various errands, picking up after each stop, and going on where he had left off. It was more about Gamel than Hetty – about the strangeness of their marriage and the ways in which he found it unsatisfactory; chiefly the lack of warmth and affection. 'I must have warmth and love. I'm very good-humoured really,' he said. 'I never know whether Gamel's fond of me or not. I'm very fond of her, of course – I like her voice, her way of dressing, I like to see her about the garden and in the house, but . . .' The complaints were familiar: that she *did* nothing, boasted endlessly of having taught the servants to cook mashed potato but that was *all* she had taught them; that she didn't 'run the house' but left everything to him and Rosario; lived in the past – and not even the real past, but one she had invented – that she was so reserved that they could talk of nothing but their cats. I tried to make him agree how well she had taken Joanna and Hetty, with what restraint and dignity, and I think he realizes this, though he likes to think that he has given up all sorts of delights for Gamel's sake, such as going to Morocco with Hetty yet again. I pointed out that he'd had a wonderful time when he *did* go (I didn't add that it had nearly killed him) and that he'd had a tremendous lot of fun all round and Gamel hadn't interfered with his obsessions at all. Possibly he resents her passenger attitude to their joint life from a financial point of view – what does he get in return? Neither housekeeping, nor companionship, nor demonstrated affection. Yet he readily admits she rises to an emergency extremely well.

January 23rd

Gerald and I took a beautiful walk on the hillside yesterday afternoon. He immediately went back to his old monologue about Gamel and Hetty. Why had he married Gamel? he asked. But that, he said, was what marriage was like. My feeble protests drawn from the depths of an utterly different experience went unheeded or met with 'Ah, but your marriage was quite exceptionally close.' I didn't feel our conversation had led anywhere, but as if Gerald had been knitting away – or tossing himself off – in my presence; nor was anything of interest and stimulation thrown out among the lumps of lava from his volcano. Indeed, there is little said in this house to stimulate thought, and I'm beginning to crave something to set my mental life going again, as talk of Hetty or the cats does not. The cats! – ten times a day Gamel (or even Gerald) will announce that Baby, the adolescent tabby Tom, is becoming well-behaved and learning not to jump on the tables, lick all the food and plates and then have diarrhoea all over the stairs, passages and sometimes beds. Just as regularly Baby disproves this optimism by doing one of these things.

Then there's Jason, who is beyond little Teresita's[1] control. I read him *Hansel and Gretel* the other evening and after hearing how the children had put the witch on the fire he dashed off to the kitchen, seized Baby and would have done the same to him if Antonio hadn't intervened! Gamel was as nearly furious as she can be.

January 24th

Gamel remained in bed all yesterday, feverish and coughing. Conversation between Gerald and me is easier in her absence. He

---

[1] The Brenans' youngest servant, aged about thirteen.

Burgo contemplates his next move against Anthony Blond

Nicko Henderson and Boris Anrep playing chess at Ham
Spray

Lunch at Roquebrune: Julia and Lawrence Gowing,
and Burgo

Julia Gowing critically quizzes Burgo's loaded plate

David Garnett (Bunny)
and Ralph

James and Alix Strachey
on one of their annual
visits to Ham Spray

Clive Bell, and Barbara, at the Clos de Peyronnet,
waited on by Rosetta

My dear friends Clodagh (Pin) and Colin
Mackenzie having tea outside Kyle House, Skye

Janetta with her youngest daughter, Rose Jackson, on the balcony at Alpbach, Austria

David and Rachel Cecil at Cranborne, a family party; Lady Emma Cavendish, Hugh, David, Rachel, Jonathan and Laura Cecil

Lunch at Martin's fish restaurant, Malaga: Basil and Frances
Creighton, Eardley Knollys and Duncan Grant

Gerald Brenan in the 'mirador' at Churriana, Spain, paying
more attention to his own utterances than to his pretty visitor

Magouche Fielding and Janetta picnicking on our drive home from South Spain

E. M. Forster and Raymond Mortimer at Long Crichel House

Mary Dunn and Henry Bath on the terrace at Philip Dunn's house at Alcudia, Mallorca

A 'jumbo' lunch at Stokke, Wiltshire: Magouche, Lord
Jellicoe and Derek Jackson

Henrietta Partridge with her baby daughter, Sophie Vanessa

started talking about Carrington again, and produced three fat packets of her letters which I read far into the night and finished reading this morning. I'm glad I did: I found them enthralling and extraordinarily good as letters. I became fascinated afresh by her personality – something close to genius – which poured itself out so freely in these long, original, poetical and amusing letters that there was not much left to go into her painting, or even her conversation. And whence came the violence of her dislike of children (and marriage too) and resolution never to have any? Was that Lytton's influence? I'm sure this dread of losing Lytton was the operative factor in most of the major actions of her life – marrying Ralph, for example. Lytton wanted her to. Might she even have gone off with Gerald had it not been for him? That she was the active one in their affair was very plain. But when the chain of circumstances and human behaviour is spread out before one it is impossible to guess how important each link is in the chain, how easily things might have gone differently.

The excellence of Carrington's letters has made me rather discontented with Desmond's, and I'm growing to be doubtful whether they'll really make a book.

Before she took to her bed Gamel asked my advice as to what she should do with the correspondence between herself and Llewelyn Powys – love-letters between a great man and his Egeria; 'perhaps his best work', and hinted at others from Bertrand Russell. 'Perhaps they should be given to some American University?' Her brother had already sent her war letters written to him to one of them. I hope the little boast reassured her.

January 26th

Two marvellously lovely days and Carrington's letters to Gerald have swept me along, with no time (mercifully) to look right, left or in front. They have interested me enormously, perhaps especially since I got to the period when my love-affair with Ralph began. She seems to have been marvellously unresentful and unjealous, marvellously able to fall a little in love with innumerable people as well as cats, birds, and what she called 'visions' or 'images' of the outside world. And a letter I read last night gives one clue. She hated being a woman; her sexual feelings were really very unimportant. What she loved was the mingling of personalities, she loved people too for their appearance or 'literary' value, couldn't forgive them for being ugly. And she always became resentful when one of her lovers made sex of prime importance in their relation. She explains this to Gerald – in 1925 I think it was – when she felt unable to respond to him physically because he set such store by it, and said that this was what had made her relation with Mark Gertler and Ralph so difficult. 'Since Ralph had ceased treating her as a woman they'd got on much better.' This, I think, explains her lack of resentment at my carrying him off. Also this *un*womanliness explains her horror of children and maternity, and the intense pain and gloom (always referred to at length) heralding her monthly periods and accompanying them, something now thought often to be psychological.

Janetta will soon be here, but I think very little about the future, my flat, London, Burgo, for it is still an unscripted area.

January 27th

Curious effect of reading, as an appendix to the Carrington letters, some drafts of letters from Gerald to her – her own letters left me feeling her a golden character, remarkable, a near genius. From these agonized scrawls of Gerald's one detected the other side of the picture – that she would never quite let him go, yet couldn't help tormenting him. Taken any way it was a moving tragedy. Yet had they, for instance, gone off together after Watendlath,[1] what would have come of it I wonder? Very little in terms of duration, I believe. For the fact was she was most loving when the object was unattainable – Gerald when banished to Spain, and (all her life) Lytton. I felt much moved when I came to the packet marked 'Last Letters', and read two she had written after Lytton's death, and then my own telegram: 'Carrington died today. Can you come. Will meet you anywhere.'

January 28th

I thought that the Carrington letters were all read and that this chest full of the past (whose lid I had lifted, peering into what it

---

[1] The hamlet near Keswick in the Lake District where Gerald and Carrington had first fallen in love.

contained) was now shut down. But last night Gerald found four-teen consecutive missing letters of hers and one of Ralph's, which, had they been discovered by a biographer writing about the Byrons or the Carlyles, would have been thought 'very important indeed'. They revealed that the crucial moment in the quadrangular situation (Gerald – Carrington – Ralph – me) was in January 1924 when I spent a week in Paris with Carrington and Ralph, who were on their way back from their second Yegen visit. Ralph's letter to Gerald mentions the possibility of 'going off with F.'

At the same time Carrington had been writing from Paris her most loving, promising, encouraging letters to Gerald, letters which might have induced him to hope for anything he wanted when he came to England later that year. 'Ralph will be happy with Frances,' she seems to say. 'Why shouldn't you and I . . . ?' Then came the letter from Ralph I have just mentioned, and Carrington opened it. She told Gerald she 'read' it, and it's clear he hadn't meant her to, also the envelope has plainly been torn and clumsily stuck down. So the researcher into the past can follow that her subsequent behaviour followed directly from her having read there Ralph's suggestion that he might leave her for me. There is a *complete* withdrawal of promises to Gerald, a retraction into herself, and a pathetic panic, filling pages on end with fears lest he should write something that Ralph might resent. As Ralph said, 'No-one will ever know' what part he, or Ham Spray, or Lytton took in the whole conglomerate of the life she feared to lose, but did fear desperately. Well, she did gradually, I think in the years between 1925 and 1932 when Ralph and I were living in London, realize that she *wasn't* going to be utterly bereft, and I think she gained confidence thereby. Looking back, I think the solution we found was a civilized one.

Another walk with Gerald up the hill to the firs. We found several fritillaries in bud and one nearly out. I like talking to Gerald – much, much more than I like talking to Gamel – but he's oddly unstimulating, like a girl-friend in youth. Very few people's conversations really stimulate – both the Gowings do, Robert and Janetta; no-one, of course, as Ralph did. And no-one will ever make me laugh as he did.

O Gamelismus! I did laugh inwardly yesterday at the way she brought out faded passport photographs of Powyses, or others of houses of no possible significance in Charleston and views in the mystic South, hoping by these totem objects to prove that she too had a significant past among the illustrious.

By giving me Carrington's letters to read, Gerald has done me a great service: he has made me think more freely and realistically, and this has come about by means of starting with a period which was prehistoric – before my time, and gradually developing through the drama we all shared to the more or less settled compromise life right up to Carrington's death. My historical interest in seeing things I lived through from the other side has carried me along and the result has been not only that I am the wiser about certain things in the past but a certain catharsis has spread its benign force and warmth, invading areas of more recent pain. I am again really grateful to Gerald; I don't know how much of this was deliberate, or *why* exactly he wanted me to read the letters, but he has done me a service, yes.

A telegram from Janetta that she hopes to arrive tonight. I'm longing to see her, and having done so I shall know more about my own immediate future.

January 29th

What pleasure to see Janetta's sweet face peep round the door of the sitting-room where we were sitting over the fire. She was followed closely by Magouche and both of them brought a current of familiarity (ideas, words that one is at home with) into the house, which had been topsy-turvy with the presence from about two till six-thirty of Hetty and three other beatniks, who all sat in the roof-room throughout the radiant afternoon in a mystic circle like the mice in Edward Lear's *Nonsense Book*, drinking montilla, smoking marijuana and jabbering inanely. I found it pleasanter to read Peter Rabbit books to poor Jason, who was unsettled by the electric atmosphere of impending change.

We're off tomorrow, and like Jason, I'm unsettled so I can't write.

February 7th: London, West Halkin Street

So here I am, have been for two nights in my so-called nest, and thank heaven it even has a slightly home-like feeling. Certainly I felt none of the repulsion for it I did before I left. I think Spain was a relief – there was company without a taxing strangeness, there was the curious catharsis from returning to the past, there was the effect simply of side-stepping out of my groove. And I suppose it should be comfort of a sort to find that it happens so, and presumably would again. I have been busy all of these two days settling myself in in various ways. I think I've engaged an admirable Scotch body as weekly help. I trust my impressions, and I swear she's what I want.

Last night Burgo came round for a drink. He was perfectly inscrutable, not unduly cast down I'd say, but I don't even know that – and I found myself wondering what on earth he feels for me. I know no-one who succeeds so totally in veiling his persona from view, and heaven knows what goes on in his head. His most forthcoming remarks, which led to a 'real' discussion, were about criticism being a low form of activity, like advertising.

Well, here I am, and I'm trying to harness myself between the shafts of this life.

The Janetta journey was tougher than the Eardley one. We drove often longer into the night, there was more recklessness, less middle-aged safeness. Our last morning we drove all out at seventy miles an hour average to catch the one o'clock aeroplane at Calais, having miscalculated the distance. At Toledo we separated temporarily, and I went alone and sat in front of the Count d'Orgaz, reflecting that it was one of the most splendid pictures in the world, and that one reason for this was that it drew its vitality from an emotional and philosophical attitude to the transition from life to death just as requiems do, so often the best works composers produce.

February 11th: Lambourn

Sitting alone in the Gowings' oak room, church bells cascading outside; it's nearly six o'clock. I'm made a little anxious by the state of Lawrence's health. He got here before me, dead tired after a fortnight's crisis and interviews with the police over abortions and drug-taking in his art school, went to bed and the 'tickle in his throat' loomed over the household and has done ever since. At times he dashes down like a whirlwind and rushes into the cold garden to dig, then back to bed. I've had two conversations with him, one in his bedroom about Spanish pictures he seemed to enjoy, the other over downstairs lunch about the crisis at the school he didn't. Why didn't I act on the signals I saw? Following on the headlines about TICKLE IN THROAT, we now have LAWRENCE'S NOSE DEFINITELY RED AND SORE. The *fuss* that arises like steam from the faintest Gowing malaise has clouded the air as well as keeping Julia on the hop, up and downstairs with trays and preoccupation. We scurry to bed like shot rabbits as the clock strikes ten each night.

But conversation with Julia is everything I most like: always teasing away at general ideas, stimulating, amusing. A lot about writing, and some about the grievances of women – arising from Simone de Beauvoir's *Second Sex*. All the groans emitted by an unsatisfied lesbian who wants to be man as well as woman are music to Julia's ear. She feels sure women have a raw deal, and one must go easy when arguing with her because she feels it so burningly. From reading Adrian Stokes's extraordinary and poetical works we got on to the biological source of art. Stokes (following Klein) believes it to come from the desire to make reparation for the destruction achieved by the aggressive instinct – sometimes he'll put it more crudely: to put together the mother-figure he's angrily torn to pieces. Julia volunteered that for her the aesthetic impulse came from the desire to glorify and preserve experience. With which I for one don't quarrel at all. I have only one idea a month and this month's is the one about the Count d'Orgaz and requiems. I enlarge it now to include art which refers directly to other major situations in life, such as love between man and woman, such as Rembrandt's betrothal; and birth, for which one must think up some genuinely felt (not perfunctory) nativity. And also to combat abstract painting.

I have enjoyed the spare beauty of English February, a strange sight to me, not seen for five years and more, I realize. Trundling in the bus to Newbury this morning under a grey sky, I revelled in the bare trees gently cooked brown at their tips, clumps of snowdrops among dark ivy leaves, white surface of streams brushed by the wind and the *velvet* texture of everything from donkeys and horses to the short pale grass.

February 13th: West Halkin Street

I was anxious of course about my return, and now that a whole week has gone I'm nervously wondering whether it's really safe to say I am 'better', or whether I shall fall suddenly through some ghostly elephant-trap into a deep hole of despair, or that like a woman in childbirth I will again experience the return to hideous pain when my hand slips from the gas-machine.

Meanwhile I can only grasp greedily – as she does – at relief of any sort, even if it is fictitious; and I'm thankful that for the moment I am not rejecting everything, as a telephone-box rejects foreign or worn coins.

February 21st

I am making strenuous loops as with a giant crochet-hook to fasten myself to the outside world. One loop is a series of violin lessons with a friend of Kitty West's,[1] a Hungarian once a child prodigy and now a self-possessed and enthusiastic teacher. I'm also attacking the *technique* of being alone. I force myself to spend quiet evenings by myself, as I have just done now – working till dinnertime, then listening to the wireless and reading. My violin teacher tries to make me think of my left hand as if it were moulding a lump of clay; I feel that in a more violent and effortful way that is what I'm trying to do to my daily life. It doesn't give me satisfaction exactly, but helps me stave off pain.

I've seen two curious characters about Desmond's letters – Enid Bagnold,[2] a brisk youthful and handsome seventy-year-old, running round on high heels, cooking chicken with rosemary, remembering apparently without effort, displaying her charm, dealing with dogs and grandchildren. She looked rather younger than the lumbering but amiable Simon Asquith[3] (who is under forty) with his massive features and shock of grey thick hair, who tottered up my steps,

[1] Kato Havas.
[2] Writer (Lady Jones).
[3] Son of Lady Cynthia.

swallowed two whiskeys in the twinkle of an eye, left a pile of letters and tottered away. Enid Bagnold told me she was planning a novel about growing old (quite a good subject it might be) in the form of a sort of diary.

March 9th

My days have suddenly become congested with events – I have things to do far ahead. Should I hitch up (as I hope to) with an orchestra, there will seem few evenings in the week. Music is in the ascendant – I read quiet books which send me to sleep, see no pictures, go to no theatres; but opera, wireless and concerts, and also my lessons with my little Hungarian preoccupy me. Shall I go for a week to her Dorset Music Summer School? I'm tempted. Can I scoop any recollections out of the swarm of things past?

One day last week I drove to Golders Green to dine with Lionel[1] and Margaret Penrose. Jonathan,[2] the English chess-champion, was rather silent and morose. He's trying for his Ph.D. with a thesis on thinking. Lionel, given the smallest opportunity, talked about chromosomes and showed them to me through a very light elegant microscope. Stained a pretty lavender-pink, there they were in double hanks tied round the waist, chromosomes from the blood or tissue of a child, before my very eyes. I could have listened to his exposition of normal and abnormal chromosomes for ever, and under his tutorship soon began to see which patterns were abnormal. He says there is no cure for Mongolism in spite of what the newspapers say.

March 10th

Last night I went to Bunny's seventieth birthday party, a curious mixture of seventeen- and seventy-year-olds. Duncan doesn't make one think at all of age. But Arthur Waley, yes: *he* had made a great stride towards it, and the first thing he said to me was that Beryl[3] had died a few days ago; then he went on to talk compulsively of the savage cruelty of Irish hospital nurses. But he'd man-

[1] Galton, Professor of Genetics.
[2] Their youngest son.
[3] De Zoëte, with whom Arthur had lived for many years.

aged to preserve her from them and look after her himself. Now he felt utterly exhausted. A stocky figure with a snow-white head turned out to be Noel Richards – it surprised Janetta to know that she had been beloved of Rupert Brooke and James and lots of others.

March 14th

Julia on the telephone, talking about poor old Pippa,[1] nearly ninety, having 'a leg swollen to the thigh with arthritis' and unable to fend for herself or be fended for at home. Julia has had to arrange for her to go to hospital today, but Pippa is resentful and looks bitterly at her – 'It's always the same,' said Julia, 'Tommy used to be like that – the dog bites you as you're letting it out of the trap.' Then, on a surprisingly harsh note: 'I can't think why she didn't finish herself off before it got so far.'

March 21st

I haven't fallen right through any elephant-traps lately – though there have been moments when the texture of my life has worn extremely thin. I suppose the healing influence of time is in some way making itself felt. I battle on. One battle I'm pleased about is with my violin – I have, I think, fixed up an orchestra for after Easter, and this after as nearly as possible abandoning the whole thing.

April 10th

Just back from a walk in Green Park, taken both as exercise and to watch the spring. I did enjoy almost lustfully the swelling buds and cheerful twittering of the few birds, and I came back a little refreshed but unable to tell what I'd thought about. Last night at the Memoir Club, Dermod[2] talked to me about the death of small children and told me that they sometimes realized they were dying and this was agonizing to watch. Some behaved with unheard-of stoicism – in others the knowledge that they were dying made them turn violently against their parents. Someone had to be to

[1] Strachey, her aunt.
[2] MacCarthy, younger of Desmond and Molly's two sons and a doctor.

blame. This surprised and moved me. I asked him if he got at all hardened to the situation. He said quite the reverse. Enjoyable Memoir Club. Everyone came; my arrangements[1] worked, and Bunny read a short but brilliant paper about Robert Graves, Geoffrey Phibbs and Laura Riding's attempted suicide.

April 16th: Stokke

Reading D.H. Lawrence's *Letters* – what a phenomenon! Before he became a puff-adder or poisonous toadstool ejecting hate, there was (at twenty-one) something quite extraordinarily mature, original and even well-meaning in him. What exactly went wrong and made him so full of venom? During the First War he seems to have been *literally* mad. His personality obsesses me – I relate it to everything I see and hear, and too many theories which seem to explain it occur to me. His Messiah-complex and fury because the world didn't respond as if he was Jesus Christ. But the sad thing is that he should have become warped and stunted (even though so productive) after such an early and dazzling maturity.

We are an all-female household here at Stokke – Mary, Magouche and Janetta with their little girls. On Sunday Mary came with me to call on the Elweses at Ham Spray – came staunchly, dressed in black leather and prepared, I could see, to support me through all sorts of reactions I didn't in fact have. Why didn't I? I've had more of a pang catching sight of the downs and Bull's Tail[2] from afar; it's often the little unexpected thing which strikes to the heart like a fine stiletto. I was thinking mostly about the Elweses when I arrived, hoping they were happy and didn't regret, feeling responsible even for the icy weather. Did I put some pad of anaesthetic to my heart, so that I felt detachment and interest?

April 18th

To *Tristan* with Mary last night – a VAST experience, more like being subjected to a natural upheaval than a work of art; like being a rock over which break (one after another) small wave, small wave and then *huge* wave – working up to rhythmical crises.

---

[1] I was secretary.
[2] A beech hanger on the downs.

Like the copulation of elephants these crises take an eternity to come to climax. I did feel, though, 'I am enjoying this', especially in the second act; and hardly ever – but sometimes – 'Oh, we've had enough of this. Do get along to something else.' Woke in the night with a migraine and its dull echo still lingers. It's dark and gloomy and raining and I'm sunk pretty low in depression of a negative sort. I shall miss Janetta and our almost daily telephone talks, *very* much indeed.

April 26th

A lot in a sense has 'happened' but I'm doubtful how much I have extracted from it. I don't give myself time, but hurry on compulsively to the next thing. I went to the Gowings for Easter and another week is almost past since then. On Easter Day there came a sudden stunning explosion into spring. I have a confused memory of two long and beautiful walks with Julia over the rolling hill-fields just bloomed to velvet with a soft green, a pale sky of misty blue above us, a little negress with woolly hair, and her black hands eagerly thrust among white violets on a bank.

I drove the Coldstreams down, Bill[1] and his pregnant Monica. She is an Irish redhead, an ex-Slade-model. Her pregnancy made her adopt an Epstein-like attitude with her head thrust forward and her hands clasped protectively over her stomach. Bill is a very charming, intelligent fellow, active-minded, articulate, curious about everything, and with strange hankerings after Establishment values. One morning at breakfast he and I argued along Eardley lines about the privacy of the famous. Bill was for preserving it. 'What business of theirs is Stanley Spencer's private life?' he asked. I said the question surprised me, from anyone so very much interested in other people as he was. 'Oh of course I'm neurotic about it. I dread people invading my privacy – so much so that I never write letters for fear of committing myself.' He and Lawrence talked excitedly about art, administrative and otherwise, and Bill kept bursting into infectious giggles.

Julia has taken the physicists' universe under her wing. One must not say a word against it. It is a miracle. She found fault with Leonard[2]

---

[1] Later Sir William, head of the Slade.
[2] Woolf

105

for writing about the 'sinister futility' he felt it to have. 'Didn't he realize,' she declaimed, 'that all his pleasures in life, sunlight, nature and so forth depended on it being just as it was?' 'May one not criticize it *at all*?' I cried. 'Must it be perfect in every detail? It's like saying that because your life depended on your mother you mustn't say a word against her.' But Julia very quickly takes offence if one disagrees and Lawrence becomes restive. Yet truth to tell, I find something both endearing and comic in her adoption of the starry spheres, entropy, the Brownian movement, as her special protégés; and she is always ready to start a lecture on them much in the style of her aunts and reminding me somehow of a dog walking on hind legs with a lump of sugar on its nose.

She dealt manfully and magnificently with her weekend party, provided splendid meals, and rose to the occasion when Monica Coldstream told her in a sudden flood of tears that she had been having internal pains. The poor Coldstreams returned to London before they had meant to.

The hot summery weather goes on. I am expecting six or eight people to drinks – good God, and Cyril one of them! I suppose I shall survive.

April 27th

I look back on last night with unsorted feelings. The arrival of the Master[1]: at first a crossish baby expecting to find me alone and have a literary talk, but finding Jonny[2] and Julian in occupation. I led him to my bookcase and shamelessly offered him baits to ingratiate him. He was soon on the floor, happy, with his fat legs splayed out and hair flying wildly; then his own jokes and embroidered fantasies brought twinkling geniality and he was busy signing my copy of the *Unquiet Grave*. My own tongue was tied – apart from the effort of materially seeing to my visitors' 'wants' I could *never* feel at ease with Cyril. Robin and the Godleys[3] came; Burgo brought Henrietta Garnett and rather unexpectedly they had the demeanour of a pair of lovers. I admire his good taste. 'None of my business' is my feeling but I'm not sure if Bunny and Angelica would agree.

[1] Cyril Connolly.
[2] Gathorne-Hardy.
[3] Wynne and Kitty.

April 30th

Writing in the train after Crichel. Morgan[1] lay at his manifest ease in Raymond's 'pram' letting the delicate skin of one cheek scorch to a clownlike scarlet in the sun, while his rolling head directed his kind pale eyes like the beams of a lighthouse on person after person, charged with sympathetic interest. He does make the impression of *enormous* humanity and tolerance. Eardley's new friend Mattei Radev was there, an enigmatic but handsome Bulgarian with thick cream-coloured skin and a black shock of hair over the trapezium of his forehead. Raymond was applying himself almost too assiduously to the great man's comfort, irritating Eardley, shouting (too loud for Morgan's very slight deafness) the terribly over-simplified remarks the deaf have to put up with. We were bathed in sun the whole weekend; we sat in it; I walked and picked cowslips, primroses and bluebells in it; we played croquet on a lawn of the tenderest green. On Sunday night after Morgan had left us, the other four of us went to dinner with Cecil Beaton, embowered in red plush, rose-covered chintzes and silver-framed photographs. I liked all but the last and was amused by Cecil's slow but pungent remarks. ('He's always been unlucky – had his lovers *shot* under him' and so on.) I gallop round like a fairly tired horse bracing myself to take jump after jump: the five-barred gate, then the water-jump: and more lie behind.

An evening with Burgo and Henrietta at *Tosca*; Simon Asquith on Tuesday. A stretch of peace such as this offered by the train I am in ought to be used for thought, but instead I snatch at it to go into a coma of relaxation. In my new life all my thinking is done under pressure of circumstances, as if I were a lorry-driver at the wheel, and words flow from my mouth insufficiently matured, drawing up old thoughts from the depths by threads of invisible cotton.

May 7th

My second visit to Belgrave Square garden, a privilege Mary's kindness and a cheque for £10 got me. Is it worth it? Doubtful. I'm trying to enjoy as much as possible the noble black-trunked

---

[1] E.M. Forster.

trees, the gentle twittering in the bushes and the fact that I'm sitting on a seat surrounded by grass. But the flower-beds are miserably kept up and the traffic whirling round the square makes a distracting noise. The other improvement I had set my heart on embellishing my life with, my radiogram, came last week, and I am delighted with it. I'm practising listening to music *alone*, which I thought would be more difficult than it is.

To Charleston for the weekend. At Victoria there was a crowd of small boys going back to school. I can't forget one poor little crimson, drenched, quivering face, nor the brisk, unreal voice of his probably desperate mother, saying, 'Got your ticket? GOOD.'

Alas, it rained and rained quietly and wettingly all Saturday and Sunday, and I was cooped up with Clive, Duncan and Barbara in a very stuffy room. Through the window the greenish veil of rain turned the garden rapidly greener and merged the drooping willow branches with the green water. Through the green gauze of this driving mist the strange female statue they have set up on the further bank of the pond leaned forward, gazing at us and looking curiously like Vanessa herself or the spectral governess in the *Turn of the Screw*.

I spent my time searching more slowly than I need have through Clive and Vanessa's boxes of letters[1] and coming away with quite a good haul – some twenty-five. Clive was wonderful at answering questions and I think enjoyed doing so. We had delightful conversation. I'm not sure if Desmond would have allowed it to be the 'good talk' he loved to record. Lindy Guinness, the twenty-year-old rich girl who is a pupil and friend of Duncan's, came to tea. She's very pretty, friendly and confident.

May 12th: Stowell[2] (The Tycoonery)

Magouche and I came down by train. Things one does with her are never dull, have lots of flavour. We talked and laughed all the way, and ran into Lord Jellicoe who was amusing and lively too. At the end they produced a Rookery Nook situation by each

---

[1] I was still editing Desmond MacCarthy's letters.
[2] House of Philip Dunn, generally known as 'The Tycoon', who had been Mary's first husband. There was a question of their re-marriage, which later took place.

taking the other's identical suitcases away with them. I was looking forward to exceptional comfort and a lot of peace and quiet. 'We'll have breakfast in bed,' Magouche and I said to one another. But when we went up to bed, we were asked to come down in dressing-gowns about nine. All these servants, and an elderly lady can't breakfast in bed? I've got up and dressed – but I envy Magouche who has had the sense to lie low, breakfastless. Now I must get a walk by myself *coûte que coûte*. I shall plunge myself whenever possible in work.

Later (quarter to seven); the day so far hasn't gone badly. A picnic was forestalled by the dank uncertain weather. I went off for a walk along the canal by myself, a necessary freshener and stabilizer; we've just had another communal one in a bluebell wood. Last night we had Jeremy Fry and his wife Camilla to dinner – both had a good deal of charm. Later in the evening Philip came and sat amiably beside me on the sofa, but in answer – or rather, *not* in answer – to a question of Magouche's about new places for travel being 'opened up', he burst out that he didn't want more places opened up, the desirable thing was to close them down – make them accessible to the lucky few, and return to a civilization of 'individuals' not masses, etc., etc. I said I thought it true that at present the masses didn't much enjoy exotic places, but in time education would make them more able to. Philip: 'Education doesn't do any good, only standards handed down from parents to children.' F: 'That *is* education – and when the present young are educated and have been to universities they'll be better qualified to educate their own children.' Philip: 'There are no universities now, only technical colleges.' F: 'Oh, come now, there are several new ones being built – Brighton, for instance.' Philip: 'They're not real universities: they don't *discuss* in them.'

I remained very mild during this interchange (I say this on Magouche's evidence who was amazed that I did – for there was more that was provocative which I've forgotten). My theory is that he deeply disapproves of both Magouche and me, but as we've both been too polite to try and aggravate him by putting forward views he wouldn't like, he's been reduced to attacking the views he knows we hold. That's been quite annoying enough for him. Poor fellow, he's ghastly bored, restless, doesn't know what to do with himself. His one idea is (like all millionaires) to fill in his time with toys and games (cards, croquet, ping-pong) and with trying desperately to keep his body as trim as possible. He has heated up his swimming-pool and in spite of the cold of the day insists on swimming in it; he goes riding every morning. And what's it all for?

At breakfast Philip said to Seton (another guest): 'I said so many things to shock Frances last night,' (smiling pleasantly). F: 'Did you think I seemed shocked? I don't think I did. You were trailing your coat a bit, but I don't think you got a rise out of me.' This was talking his own language, though also true, so he liked it and laughed, and now wants to take me out 'to look at some churches'.

May 14th

All yesterday Philip laid himself out to be agreeable to me and of course I was mollified. Ping-pong: Baths to lunch (Henry Bath is a very amusing character: Virginia was unable to talk to the Tycoon any better than anyone else).

There! I've been up to my tricks again – unconsciously in this case, I do believe, while criticizing the Tycoon I must have been 'trying to make him like me'. Mary rang up today to say that I had succeeded so well that he's keen for me to go and stay in Majorca this summer and 'would gladly pay my fare'.

May 23rd

Nothing but a few flashes are left from last weekend at Lawford: a lot of people laughing at jokes. Puffin Asquith[1], cause of the amusement, walking at his ease round the room with his pale snout-shaped face tilted on one side, bringing out a chain of stories, his own laughter deliberately checked on an indrawn gasp like a dying horse. Then – walking with him and Phyllis on the marshes in an ice-cold easterly wind of great violence, Rocco the pointer wildly lolloping through a green sea of young wheat, Phyllis and Puffin capping each others' quotations from Victor Hugo – always with the assumption 'of course you remember'. Weeding with Phyllis – a nice interlude producing a sense of companionship. Phil in a sudden burst of euphoria saying that every house ought to

[1] Anthony, film director.

have three things – children, dogs and a piano – otherwise it's not a proper house. Rocco the dog certainly comes first in this house, and when he hurt his paw he took the centre of the stage completely.

Other guests at Lawford – a couple of successful New Zealanders, *vin* very *ordinaire*; also Vivien John and her husband. Puffin Asquith is a professional charmer, too professional to show he knows he's charming.

Last night I fell gently asleep after a happy orchestral evening, thinking sadly along well-travelled lines – about the thoughtlessness produced by living as a singleton. With Ralph alive, any chance reflection of either his or mine would by the very fact of communication be developed and patted to and fro, leading perhaps to the exploration of a whole new region of ideas; to fun, sudden glimpses down by-roads. But what happens now? Any seed of a general idea I may have drops to the ground, and is blown away. It takes two to think.

May 30th

Clive, Boris and Maud Russell dined with me last night. I believe they all enjoyed themselves, and the only difficulty was that Clive's punctuality neurosis prompted him to arrive three-quarters of an hour early, an uncertain expression on his face at my door, saying, 'I've come to see if I can be of use.'

I'm in the Square garden again, bathed in restorative sunlight, while three tiny Spanish boys run about with their woolly coats over their heads, roaring like lions.

June 6th

Yesterday I went to tea with Bobo Mayor[1] – white-haired, gasping with asthma, but how charming, looking at me with her bright black intelligent eyes. I liked her enormously, and over tea from a thermos we exchanged the stories of our lives and nibbled sweet biscuits.

In the evening a dinner-party at Maud Russell's – Peter Quennell, the Connollys, the Lennox Berkeleys, Boris, Patrick Kinross, the

---

[1] Beatrice – playwright, and an early love of Clive's.

Baroness Budberg. Lennox Berkeley and I talked about abstract art. With Boris it was suicide; he wore his most corrupt, endearing, tobacco-stained Moujik smile. 'Where is the difficulty?' he said. 'One dies every night when one goes to sleep. It is only necessary to see one doesn't wake up; take more pills than usual – if that doesn't work, take a few more. But one must die quietly and pleasantly – not like the Nazis, gasping and choking and writhing with prussic acid.' The self-consciously 'good talkers' at the table were Peter Quennell and Cyril. Peter soon turned his back on Deirdre Connolly, by-passed the Budberg, and shouted across to Cyril at the opposite corner of the table. An answering sparkle and smile came back from Cyril – indeed, they talked to each other most of the evening and the wonder is that two such egotistical talkers will hear each other out enough to stimulate each other. Towards the end of the evening these two literary pundits came and sat each side of me – the poor slice of ham in their sandwich – on the sofa. The subject was literary of course (Desmond) and I felt their benevolence flooding down on me as from twin bedside lamps. Indeed, both were markedly genial, though for some reason I find this as embarrassing as the opposite would be.

The suicide talk arose from something which happened in the morning. When good Mrs Ringe let herself in at my door there was a man's voice with her. She came to me later and told me she'd 'had to bring her husband'. He was terribly upset because the man who lived opposite had hanged himself last night; he was a great friend, they saw him every day, and his wife had come to them for help when she couldn't unfasten the door. They were there when a policeman had broken it in and told them they'd better keep away. Mrs Ringe's face as she told me expressed all the humanity, the good taste, the kindness that's in her character. She's a wonderful woman, and I love her dearly.

Bunny came to lunch with me the other day. From his talk he showed that he knew there was an attachment between Burgo and Henrietta, and doesn't mind it. In fact he seems glad, and rejoiced my heart by saying that Henrietta said 'Burgo was *the kindest man in the world*'.

June 19th

Last night to Tippett's opera *King Priam*, with Rosamond[1], whose opinion of the work I shared more than I can her preoccupation with death and the next world. I find the old theme of Troy – Paris, Hector, Helen, Achilles – about as moving as Henty boys' books. Heroes leave me very cold. Have been reading *Troilus and Cressida* for a more sympathetic view of these characters – particularly of Hector.

All day I had been tidying-up the Desmond position. I wrote to Michael[2] suggesting that three days' or so hard work 'on the spot' was necessary but it wasn't too late if he wanted to back out. I haven't an idea what he'll say, but I half hope he will want to drop it, for I feel discouraged about it. Meanwhile Gollancz has asked me to revise a Spanish translation – and this I've said I'll do next month, whatever Michael's answer. They have also offered me another Spanish book to translate afterwards; I'm half tempted, half afraid. My confidence is only up to my ankles – in every department, work, violin, driving my Mini. I drove it to the Tate to see the Francis Bacons this afternoon. *Well* – they are very impressive of course.

June 24th: Aldeburgh

Aldeburgh – or rather, a pleasant little inn in the village of Westleton, eight miles away. Janetta and I have been for two days engulfed in the mild salt Suffolk air; vast sky, huge elms, churches too large and fierce for their villages but softened by thatched roofs, grey sea washing in over steep shingle densely matted with purple sea-pea and yellow stone-crop, heathy commons smelling of broom and gorse. The Aldeburgh festival itself is dominated by hero-worship for 'Ben', who has only to appear waving a Prince Charming hand for the audience to be convulsed by applause. Janetta and I were to some degree in rebellion against the no-criticism decree, and perhaps went in for too much of it.

Sociological aspects of the Festival centre round the Gathorne-

---

[1] Lehmann.
[2] Desmond's eldest son had carried off most of his father's literary and personal letters.

Hardys and their Queen Bee.[1] When we went to dinner there, Janetta completely won the old lady round in the most magical way. There is a charming humanity and intelligence, and responsiveness also, coming from Lady Cranbrook's grey eyes. Bob was there rattling away like a machine-gun. I was asked several times by him or his mother, 'Have you ever seen *Tillaea muscosa?*'[2] and told the story of how it had been found close to Snape church. It became a sort of absurd refrain, and (as I remembered the same had happened on both my previous visits) I was glad to stop on the way home and find the little thing.

Night thoughts were about Art and Beauty. The second of these seemed irrelevant at the Bacons. 'How ever did we come to value Art?' I asked myself, beginning to unpick and go right back to the start, then taking up the threads again when I woke in the small hours. 'Biological bait' were the words that came into my mind, or they may have been there before, certainly the notions they represent have: that we call 'beauty' what attracts us to get our biological ends – the ripe red of a strawberry, the bloom of a young skin – but that art consists in cultivating these attractions for their own sake, just as skating may have begun as a means of crossing a river, but from the pleasure in their skill people worked out a means of artfully cutting figures on the ice. But where, in all this, does such impressive ugliness as that of the Bacons come in?

July 7th: Hilton

I drove here yesterday in hot summery weather. A cricket match was going on and I sat beside Bunny under an elm watching the stocky, purposeful figures, William[3] among them, while the aroma of freshly-picked strawberries rose from a basket beside us. Nothing could have been more English.

Angelica and I have had a lot of music – I at the piano, as she has returned with all her concentrated energy to the violin. I longed to have a go on hers, but it wasn't suggested. We played and played till both our faces were drained to the colour of yellowing paper. No-one would have guessed how much we had been enjoy-

---

[1]   Dorothy, Lady Cranbrook.
[2]   A very small and rare wild plant.
[3]   Garnett, Bunny's son and my nephew.

ing ourselves. She is admirably full of activities and projects, makes jam, mosaic tables, cooks delicious meals and looks beautiful. Seventy-year-old Bunny is rosy and blooming. William and the twins seem to be afloat: the sweetness of Nerissa's smile is matched by a faint but attractive ferocity in Fan's.

Sunday

Hotter still, with thunder in the air. Leaves and grass look pale and dusty with heat. Roses grow enormously fast before fading and then suddenly drop. I have been sitting at a little table outside Richard's cottage, working at my translation, an apple-tree over my head, Siamese cats prowling unhappily, a noise of busy sawing and scraping and contented voices from the twins and William engaged on making fishing-rods and catamarans, a plop as Bunny submerges his plump torso in the swimming-pool. From indoors comes the endless, almost too obsessional sound of Angelica's violin.

July 26th: London

Gerald's book – the first volume of his memoirs, came out yesterday. Looking at what he says about Ralph, I *still* feel that there is a certain maliciousness in the picture. Some element of hero-worship, as he says, but more desire to make fun of him than he's aware of and I find this hard to tolerate. He emphasizes the contrast between his attitude to pacifism in the two wars, without making it clear that it's far more respectable to think fighting justifiable when you yourself are of an age to do it and change your mind later than the reverse. The Hills at dinner last night had been reading it and I felt they were pregnant with reactions. It took very little to coax out of them that they had felt exactly as I do about the portrait of Ralph, and think it gives no notion whatever of his mental calibre.

My head's in a whirl after lunching with Rupert Hart-Davis and Richard Garnett to discuss Desmond's letters. After reading his edition of Wilde's letters I greatly respect Hart-Davis' scholarship. He's also a natural all-rounder, a Bonham-Carter almost, but does he deliberately set out to charm? He opened fire on me by telling me that he'd known and been fond of Ray.[1] 'I hold the private theory that she had been Bunny's inspiration and that he'd written nothing really good since her death.' He launched therefrom into the account of the row between them when they were publishing partners and (taking the bull by the horns) went on: 'The trouble was, of course, that it wasn't about what it was supposed to be about – which was money. He thought he was angry with me because I'd been financially a rogue, but really it was because of the unreliability of his literary judgements.'

August 3rd

Yesterday began my ten days in Dorset and yesterday too for the first time I let go of my life-line. I've gone off, that is, without my work, and it cost me some qualms and anxious fears to do so. It's something of a try-out to see if I dare do the same in Spain.

I left London bright and blue directly after breakfast, my Mini piled with coats, suitcase, fiddle and a basket in which were substitute life-lines like books, camera and wireless.

August 12th

The object of my journey was to spend a week at Kato Havas' music school at Langton Maltravers. What a mistake! I felt I was back at boarding-school. I only hope it hasn't cured me of wanting to play the violin. I put up in a small local hotel and kept my afternoons strictly to myself. The thing that gave me most pleasure was finding the rare Dorset Heath; I got none at all from my fellow-musicians. As for Kato she was bent on divesting us one and all of any technique we had acquired – particularly *vibrato*. The experience was unnerving in the strangest way and I returned to my little old flat with relief. Steadiness is now my sole aim: I dread a return of that quavering of the spirit. The human *vibrato* seems to have nothing to be said for it.

As I waited for a bus yesterday, London was an inferno, ugly in sight and sound, with angrily-crashing gears, macs and brollies and plastic bootees, and diagonal shafts of rain. Yet, how odd it is, disengaged as I am from life, rejecting and 'refusing' (like a

[1] My sister and Bunny's first wife.

116

horse at a jump), I find I am suddenly capable of receiving a rare breath of excitement from the beauty of a dark tree against the white stucco front of a house with a lighted window in it; also the dusky feverishly-illumined night sky of London with a great cheesy moon hanging in it.

Cyril came to have a drink with me two nights ago, and I'm glad that I decided to take him undiluted. I grow to like *tête-à-tête* conversations more and more; nearly everyone is at their best when not schizophrenically divided between various listeners on whom they want to make different impressions. Guards were lowered, a sort of *rapport* established, and Cyril seemed at his ease with me as never before. I have always admired his intelligence and imagination and he's almost the only person to whom I would apply the word 'wit'. But this time I also liked him. There was a free and easy moment when he was seized with a cramp in his side and hurled himself back into a chair and undid his trouser buttons. Having read some letters from him to Desmond I had realized that he had, as a very young man, been in love with Racie Buxton.[1] Tentatively I remarked that I had gathered that he had been fond of Racie. '*Fond* of her? I was *madly* in love with her!' He told me he had been until then exclusively homosexual and this was a shattering and new experience. Patrick Kinross had at the same time got attached to Racie's sister Ros. Desmond had been very understanding, Rachel kind and helpful, but Molly adamantly obstructive. As a result of which Racie's parents were told that their daughters' young men were both 'upside down', or homosexual in MacCarthy language, and they were forbidden to meet. Cyril resents to this day (and I think with justification) not that they were forbidden to marry, but that the relationship was thus forcibly nipped and broken, instead of being allowed to flower and develop. So that he always felt deprived, and even though he fell in love with Jean[2] soon after, she felt that it was on the rebound – she was a substitute Racie.

---

[1] Horatia, niece of Molly MacCarthy.
[2] His first wife.

August 21st: Alhaurin, Spain

The shock of change, and the confusion of some of the last two days has been great. On Sunday I was lunching peaceably with Isobel and sitting in her London garden listening to the Sunday English chatter over the wall. That same evening at nine-thirty I left the ground on my way to Spain,[1] and nearly all the way, if I cared to look out from my window in the tail of the aeroplane, I saw towns and villages spangled below – sometimes in evil shapes like sinister sprawling insects. Only now, aloft in this mysterious transition, did I begin seriously to project myself into the next few weeks. Bump and swerve – poor landing – we were down, and as I walked across the field, I could see haloed against the footlights figures waving, whether at me or not I couldn't tell. Yes – there were Georgie's marvellous long brown legs in shorts, Rose, Janetta's neat head, Jaime,[2] Joanna Carrington (just off back to England) and Gerald.

By the time we reached Janetta's house at Alhaurin it must have been 3 a.m. and all the way in the car my intoxicated nose drew in strange musky smells, maquis-like, indefinable smells of heat, while in the headlights I saw the brittle brownness of the Spanish grass. The shock of arrival was stupendous – the breathless moonlit walls, mountains still magically clear and sharp with a starry sky behind, the balmy odoriferous warmth.

Janetta and I sat by the swimming-pool talking for an hour and still I couldn't believe I was really here and hadn't the smallest desire for sleep or feeling of fatigue.

All ordinary rules of life are in abeyance here. It will be a pleasure to discover the new ones. The heat by day is intense, and the *only* way to keep cool is to get into the swimming-pool at least every hour or so. Georgie and Rose are there all the while. Last night I couldn't sleep till I had stolen out in the darkness and submerged myself in the tepid water. One is alert, rather stimulated all the time; the heat is so violent it's nearly an enemy.

I have the Southbys' very grand bedroom with a vast triple bed. Janetta prefers the book-room; there are two fine bathrooms, very civilized. This is the stage on which who knows what *dramatis*

---

[1] To stay with Janetta and her family in this charming rented house.
[2] Parladé, shortly to marry Janetta.

personae may shortly appear. As for me, I am relaxed and content, in the physical delight this place engenders.

August 22nd

Yesterday the heat loomed over everything: one could think of nothing but how to keep cool. It advanced, stated itself, 'here I am', and increased steadily and inexorably like the blare of an enormous trumpet, an advancing army, till all one's thoughts were for survival.

In the evening we went to pick up the Brenans to bring them back to dinner – their patio was crowded with people in the darkness among the lamplit trees, as if we were all in a room with very dark wallpaper and a party going on – Miranda,[1] Xavier and two children, Freddie Wiseman and various young men (all 'poets' to Gamel).

Gerald is terribly thin, and his look of exhaustion is quite alarming. As I turn over last night in my mind I'm filled with indignation at the way Gamel contradicted him every time he opened his mouth: 'No, it wasn't like that *at all*,' and 'Don't be funny.'

August 24th

Janetta went to Torremolinos to fetch Jaime. Later we were joined by Georgia Tennant and Nicky, Julian and a friend, so the house is now quite full, but with no sense of permanency about it. I am aware that plans are being rapidly and hectically developed, but can only guess what they are.

Janetta and Jaime have vanished again, and I find myself vaguely in charge of the two boys and the four girls. We have two lovely and efficient maids but as they too have not been kept informed, Paca greeted my explanations with agitation. She couldn't understand the comings and goings, the mattresses on the floor, and there had been 'mucho trabajo' ever since the Señora had arrived. This is partly because it is their pride to rise to the level of events, and they generally do.

---

[1] Corre, Gerald's daughter and her family.

August 25th

Managing rather well so far. This is no place for sleep; the air is too electric and stimulating; that familiar English drowsiness doesn't overtake one. The maids are soothed a bit, I think. However, they grasp anxiously at any indications about how many, and who and what there'll be for meals. They tell me they're off duty all Sunday afternoon – so presumably I cook the dinner.

August 28th

Janetta returned in the evening. How lovely to hear her voice, as she sat in the darkness with Jaime outside the front door. Julian and I went to call on the Brenans and got a much happier glimpse of them; without snapping and sparring. Gerald sat like a figure carved out of polished bone or an oriental sage, letting drop his original and surprising remarks. Julian's conversation is usually very lively and varied, and he's exceptionally responsive to whoever he's talking to. I must say that during the three and a bit days of Janetta's absence there had been great solidarity and co-operation in the captainless ship, Julian in particular always ready to inject his own high spirits into anybody who happened to be depressed. With Janetta's return he suddenly went to pieces. Perhaps he had felt wounded by her going as soon as he arrived and before he could get whatever he had on his chest off it. Did I write 'high spirits'? He began to give her a long account of what we had done in their absence, and burst into tears when he thought she wasn't listening. 'I was obviously boring you!' he wailed.

August 29th

I begin to write in bed, the Siamese cat lying close and rather too hot behind me. From Janetta's room, which is almost an annexe of mine, come the murmurs of her voice and the children's. From out in the garden the sound of the slow but ceaseless activity of the very, very old gardener who puts us to shame by his energy even in the heat of the day. And very hot it still is, though everyone seems to agree it has cooled off a little.

August 30th

We have had Derek Jackson with us since Tuesday evening. He dreads the heat as neurotically as he does the 'cold' water of the swimming-pool, so he stays in the darkened salon all day reading a thriller.

5.30. I was about to have a bathe before going to lunch at the Cònsula when I was bitten by a scorpion. My bathing-suit, hung from the window to dry, had fallen on to the terrace, and I picked it up and prepared to put it on. A stab of fiery pain pierced my little finger, and as I dropped my bathing-suit on the floor a horrible pinkish creature like a gamba ran out. The pain quickly burned up my arm to my armpit. What had I heard of scorpion-bites? You lose a limb? Die? Go mad? In a rather shaky voice I called to Janetta, who quickly and kindly came to my assistance. The maids, consulted, said it was best to go to the doctor for an injection, so off we went, with my finger in a tumbler of Dettol. By now I was aware I wasn't going to die at once, but the pain was bad. The doctor was fetched, and with a large crowd looking in at the windows he gave me two injections – one for the pain and another in the vein for antitoxin. I have lain on my bed and the pain has steadily diminished till it now hardly bothers me; the good doctor returned on his motor-bike and pronounced me well.

August 31st

I have had a sad letter from Gerald, who had himself weighed and found he had lost a stone since April; from this his mind was drawn irresistibly to the notions of cancer and death. Of Gamel he wrote: 'Her malady is in the mind, she disagrees with everything I say. She doesn't realize that if she had had a little more honesty with herself and with life and didn't shut herself up with her illusions she might have made more use of her talent. If I have, as I naturally suspect, a fatal disease, what I regret is that I shall not be able to look after her and Hetty.' I must try and get some conversation with him alone, but the dreaded Hetty is – alas – there now.

September 1st

I did manage to call on Gerald. Janetta dropped me while she took Derek to the airport, and I had a very human and rather touching conversation with him, sitting on the wall at the end of the garden. 'The letter I wrote you was one of those that ought never to be sent,' he began, and went on to take back some of it and then gradually replace it again. The alarming thing is Gamel's withdrawal into herself and her room, where (he thinks) she does nothing all day except say she has 'nothing to live for'.

September 4th

Five-thirty. Airborne, over the sea to Majorca. This is a small ramshackle craft, containing only about two dozen passengers and no airhostess. There was some cloud when we descended at Valencia and I was unprepared for the violent hot wind, with the breath of a furnace, blowing over the *aeropuerto*. '*Ay que calor,*' said the lavatory woman. '*Dia muy malo. Dia fatal!*'

September 6th: Alcudia[1]

The beauty of this place and the fact that it has one of the best views I ever saw came as a surprise. A long low solid two-storey farmhouse, five minutes above the sea over which it gazes from a vast terrace – a farmlike terrace, uneven and patterned with pebbles in the shape of a star; in the centre a solid prehistoric-looking stone table. Philip has made a rush roof in one corner to give shade, and there we eat. The main sitting-room also has a farmhouse character – very tall with stairs going up in the middle and painted white and royal blue. There are lots of trees, algarrobas, figs, olives, and across a narrow channel lies an island with a lighthouse. Beyond the bay the ever-changing mountains turn from bleakest grey rock to velvet. Mary met me at the airport, beaming and welcoming, accompanied by Philip's comical queer majordomo – an Englishman known as Don Carlos. She and I were alone that night, dining deliciously under the rush roof. The Tycoon arrived later with his German girlfriend Hildegarde; he

---

[1] Philip Dunn's house in Mallorca.

says she bores him stiff, but she seems now to have him more securely hooked, and as marriage to a millionaire is what she wants she may well get it.

It's nearly as hot as Malaga – too hot to sleep. Otherwise I'm happier than I expected – because of the beauty and Philip's unusual geniality. We have quantities of slaves; everything is always being tidied, and water sprinkled on the terrace to cool us. We are pampered poodles who can't possibly do a thing for ourselves, but must have any toy we want brought to us instantly. Our first day passed quietly; at night Henry and Virginia Bath arrived, with their fairylike little girl Sylvy and Derek Jackson. Yesterday we took the motor launch, loaded up with drinks and books and sun-oil, to a little bay where we bathed in crystal clear water, varying in colour from pale aquamarine to ink. The Baths seem to be a charming and united little family. Virginia is like her daughter Georgia, but where Georgia is alert, critical and ironical, Virginia is soft and yielding. Henry can be very funny in his own curious style. That mysterious fluid which after a while flows like water between any group of people has begun to circulate. I'll not be able to see it all in perspective until I'm back on my own territory. But I know I shan't forget the beauty here.

September 8th

After dinner last night Don Carlos, the major-domo, was instructed to put music on the gramophone, and strains of 'twist' music came pouring from an upstairs window down on to the terrace. Latent exhibitionism sprang to life. Henry Bath made a few wild, nostalgic movements and then refused to be decoyed onto the floor by Hildegarde, who now found her revenge by doing a slow, provocative dance in front of the men. Philip watched with sulky and inexplicit concentration. Later on she summoned Don Carlos, who came twirling and tapping out of the house, obviously ecstatically pleased to join in, and gave a charming performance.

September 13th

At lunch Philip violently attacked those intellectuals who showed how 'yellow' they were by leaving the country when war began. Derek is allowed to have his special knowledge, the arts are given their proper place, otherwise it's down with the intellectuals and up with the millionaires. Everyone is drinking more now, and Derek also had one of his epileptic outbursts about the War having been caused by the Labour Party wanting to get 'our' money away from us. The next moment he will be saying he prefers Krushchev to Kennedy and that he's practically a socialist.

I almost think it is my unvoiced protest against the values all round me that is keeping me awake at night. Virginia was inspired to say that she hated the way everyone was 'sniggering at things which are terribly sad and important', and I felt she was an ally. Yet it is so useless to argue that I don't begin.

September 11th

I was called to act as interpreter between Philip and a local carpenter-house-agent this morning from which it seemed that for more money, at a price, he is willing to sell a large part of his land for exploitation, or even – at a price again – the whole place. Much good millions do anybody! The Mallorcan suggested that he should even take over the dear little lighthouse island which lies in the centre of the marvellous view and build a bar, with dancing, '*de lujo muy caro*'. 'You're not meaning to sell this lovely place?' I asked, when the man had left. 'Well, if I'm offered enough money I MUST,' was his reply, encapsulating the philosophy of the rich.

Now I'm gloriously *alone*. All the others have gone off to Formentor in the boat to lunch with other millionaires – Whitney Straights. I'm thankful to have been allowed to stay at home.

September 19th: Lambourn

Back, morally shaken, though feeling physically strong and well. Yesterday I drove Julia down to Lambourn. The landscape inside my head is as glum and grey as what I see outside the window, or penetrated on a short icy cold walk up the road, round, back, trying unavailingly to alter my mood. I'm anxious not to disturb Julia's 'working' day, but she worries about me and I'm afraid may have realized my deep despondency. How can anyone who hasn't experienced it imagine this state of gritting one's teeth, and *enduring*, day after day, week after week? It is delightful being here though sadder than when Lawrence's optimism pervades the house. Julia talked to me about her work and I find it as usual fascinating, but she seems to be entangled in a catscradle of her own fantasies.

September 21st: West Halkin Street

The quiet, rather sad little interim at Julia's has resigned me to London. I've seen quite a lot of people in these two days, and the spectre of solitude doesn't stalk so grim.

A letter from Hart-Davis was waiting for me saying he does not think Desmond's letters good enough to publish: 'A charming person with very little to say and no great gift for letter-writing. Of course, if all his love-letters had not been destroyed the general picture might be very different.' At the same time Michael writes airily saying he has found a 'host' more letters he 'wouldn't like to tell me where'. My chief feeling is one of relief, and that it serves Michael right for trying to suppress what human interest there was. I have two jobs ahead – a Freudian index and a Spanish translation and to these I propose to devote myself.

Last night, at Janetta's. I'd rather hoped to see her alone but we had Magouche and Julian, Robert and Cynthia, Johnny Craxton in afterwards or before. A very great deal was drunk. Janetta's room was embowered in flowers: huge white lilies, freesias, gentians and small pink cyclamens. Robert gave amusing imitations of his new Independent Television venture, and when I asked him how it felt cutting his navel-string to the BBC, he replied, '*Bad*. Bleeding all over the place.'

September 24th

I think I've reached a new stage; or perhaps only realized that I ought now to embark on a new stage: and that is to live *in* my solitary London environment, to allow myself to draw a deep breath *here* in West Halkin Street, to let my foot down through the water till it rests flat, to face what my life is, and try to lead it. For with all my pride in accepting the reality-principle I have not done that hitherto. I have restlessly, feverishly, exhaustedly

125

done anything that offered, snatched up any temporary solace which would get through an hour and prevent my thinking. Why has it taken me so long to realize it?

September 29th

Enjoying Byron's life. I love his praise of Shelley: 'I never knew one who was not a beast in comparison.'

This is my second Sunday in London and I don't mind it at all, though rain is splashing steadily into the streets and I shall be alone all day. I had two musical pleasures yesterday – playing piano trios with the Penroses, and attending a splendid performance of *Wozzeck* by Hamburg State Opera. My feeling that I would grow to love this opera has now blossomed.

October 4th

A lot of scraps have gone to make my patchwork quilt lately, and some of them have been bright – even garish, but there's nothing I can spread out from it all. When Lawrence came to dinner on Monday, we sat listening to *Forza del Destino* and domestically sewing rings on a curtain to take the place of my missing door. On Tuesday Alix and James to lunch, Raymond to dinner. Talk of suicide with Raymond. He is obviously in favour of it, and thinks we all ought to have our pills. But how, he wondered, to acquire enough of them? A tentative suggestion that I should go with him to Madagascar instead of Nancy Mitford who has cried off. Went last night by myself to Sadler's Wells for Berg's *Lulu*, and found myself sitting next to Johnny Craxton. Wynne and Kitty, Joan and Paddy, and Desmond Shawe-Taylor were there.

Bad news of poor old Clive. He has to have yet another operation. For his own sake I should wish him a quiet death, but I can't for mine.

October 7th

Weekending at the Hendersons' cottage at Coombe. A wonderful gentle sunny autumn day – two, in fact. The intense pleasure I get from all my eye lights on here may be connected with the feeling that here is the country I love and belong to. The subtle curve of the valley between the downs reminds me of the one on the way to Lower Green that Ralph so loved and often commented on; the softly parting marbled roof of clouds, infinite quiet, smell of sweet decay, rusty berries in the hedges. I feel at home and at ease with Nicko and Mary.

Lying in bed, my breakfast eaten, I dreamily look at my own mental processes in aquatic terms: starting from the surface where a sheet of un-coordinated sensations lie like duckweed, one can penetrate into the depths among partly congealed ideas connected into little groups like frog spawn. Deeper still are the fundamental assumptions about values, which have sunk by sheer weight and settled on the submerged floor, sending up a stream of bubbles from time to time. I've thought a lot about individual values and how much they differ. I particularly like Bertrand Russell's 'All my life I've been convinced of the value of two things – kindness and clear thinking', to which I would add love, friendship, desire for knowledge (or curiosity, which is the same thing), peace, natural and man-made beauty, and probably many others.

While here at Coombe I've enjoyed talking to people who know a lot about public affairs and are deeply interested in them, such as Nicko and two other diplomats, Michael Stewart and a distingu-ished-looking silver-haired Frenchman called Walper. It's hard for me to keep even dimly afloat without Ralph's tuition, and I'm ashamed of my fearful blanks. The division between the arts and public affairs seems to be growing wider, and there are art-lovers who are proud of knowing and caring nothing about politics.

October 12th

I'm reading a serious historical account of 1914. It occurs to me that the ghastly waste of human courage and expense of spirit in shell-holes and mud of that time is comparable to the dreary plod of friends through their present woes, ending in the final awful stretch that so many (poor Clive, perhaps) are embarking on, and I soon shall, perhaps very soon. Two letters from Julia crashed into my consciousness this morning. She asked me to come to dinner next Monday, and thank heaven I threw up my extra night at Crichel and said I would. What has happened is perhaps worse than Julia realizes, and I can't forgive myself for critical thoughts of her. After ten years of what seemed such a happy if unusual marriage (Lawrence eighteen years her junior) which everyone has pointed to as proof that *anything* can work wonderfully well, Lawrence has burst out to Julia with the emotional admission that he has suddenly fallen in love with a girl, teacher at his school, and she with him. His proposition is that they should have a *ménage à trois* – a shattering blow and shock for poor Julia. She wrote two letters, one in utter desolation, the second pulling herself heroically together and saying that what makes Lawrence happy will make her also. She has met and likes the girl.

October 20th: Stokke

I'm staying among hearty gobblers of life who reject nothing. This Stokke weekend has fed the uncontrolled appetites of five children, a French girl and a dog, me, Julian, Tom Matthews. That's all there are at present, but today we expect Janetta, Paddy, Freddie Ayer and his wife, and Johnny Craxton. Not content with which the Gowings have been invited to dinner, and last night there was a suggestion of asking the Tycoon and all his guests to a drink. It's a frothblowers' philosophy of life – 'the more we are together the happier we shall be'.

October 21st

Yet the Jumbo form of civilization has justified itself, I must admit; and communication between so many strong personalities has turned out very stimulating, nor have I felt the need to withdraw, except after lunch when suddenly the clouds rolled back and it became clear that the most glorious hours of the day would slip by while we all sat in a cloud of tobacco haze and alcohol fumes with purpling faces. Most fascinating conversation was with Julian, who has a real talent for it. Paddy was wonderfully funny, and Freddie Ayer touching, slightly comic, and alert as a fox-terrier.

October 23rd

Further thoughts about the Jumbo weekend, or descriptions of the Gowings' visit, have all become as pointless as it seems to write any words in this book – when it now looks likely that it and us and the world itself may be blown to bits any day – perhaps tomorrow. Yesterday I worked and read till bed-time so it was not till I opened my paper this morning that any news got through and then by mortal, sinister degrees. 'Full Text of President Kennedy's Speech.' Oh! What about, pray? Cuba. (Turn to centre page: Oh well, the leader's on quite another subject so no need to take it very seriously.) But the wireless at lunch-time and this evening have forced the great heavy stone of truth down through the fogs of unwillingness.

October 24th

The impotence of our position has choked my pen. What use to put any of it into words? There's a hideous familiarity about everything, even the way that one gets used to the very horror itself.

A happier note: I've just been rung up by Burgo and went over to see him and Henrietta. What delight to see him so happy with that lovely girl and she with him; it's the best thing that ever happened to him. They've been quite alone at Bunny's cottage in Swaledale for three weeks and are as much in love as ever. More, I'd say.

October 28th: in bed at the Cecils' at Oxford

Shades of 1939 loom at times – in various ways – very large. At my orchestra on Wednesday I saw Margaret Penrose and when I crossed over to talk to her about the Cuban Crisis her intelligent round eyes grew rounder still and full of dismay. She told me Shirley[1] and all her schoolfriends were in every state from hysteria to angry tears. I thought of poor Henrietta's face yesterday and the look of real anguish that crossed it and the tears that welled into her eyes as she spoke about the stupidity of it all. I can't forget the difference between the attitudes of the young to their unique and precious lives and ours to our old done-for, worn-out ones. What's more, I feel it's to their credit they mind so much and that there's something wrong with the young who don't. They lack feeling, thoughtfulness, imagination.

The *only* good that could come out of this situation is for it

---

[1] Her daughter.

never to happen again. The last thing we should say is, 'If they could, so can we.' In that case it really was totally useless. Over and over in my head I recapitulate: one OUGHT TO MIND. OUGHT TO BE AFRAID. To be indifferent to nuclear war is nothing at all to be proud of – it is like standing unmoved in front of Goya's *Dos de Mayo*.

I met Auden for the first time at Janetta's on Friday. A delightful man, half shapeless schoolboy, half genial tortoise. He thinks Kennedy was perfectly right and when I said, 'Then shouldn't he have gone to the U.N.?' he said, 'Oh no, there was no time' – the invariable argument for making war without notice.

My fellow-guest here is called Julian Fane – author of a good little book called *Morning*. I drove him down and back in Mini, started with a very good impression of him (sensitive, intelligent, enquiring, gentle) and still hold this, yet am aware too of a conformist nature matching a tall, fine-boned, delicate-looking appearance and clothes that spoke a language of caution. David said enthusiastically, 'You're the best-dressed man I know!' from within his own dashing, spivvish clothes to this safely-dressed friend in a dark blue mac, narrow tie and black shoes. This, the language clothes speak, is what always interests me about them rather than whether they are fashionable or not.

Walking round the beautiful and extraordinarily unchanged colleges, their old grey bones draped in yellow leaves, Fane talked of Somerset Maugham, saying suddenly: 'He's an atheist and doesn't believe in a future life. Have you ever noticed how disagreeable such people are?' Obviously I didn't say I was both.

November 1st

On Monday morning the Crisis abated, with the news that Russia was prepared to withdraw the Cuban bases. Straight from the unconscious rises my death-wish, left without immediate hope of fulfilment. I see that I'm really disappointed at *not* being atomized although deeply relieved that Burgo, Henrietta, Shirley Penrose, Georgie and Rose are not. No need for logic in the Id – the most inconsistent bedfellows in the way of emotion can be found tucked in side by side.

A sharp rise of spirits last night came when Boris put in my mosaic fireplace – a glorious blazing fire and cat, so gay, so comforting, providing as it does just the elements that my flat needed that I laughed aloud and alone when I looked at it, and got so over-excited that I went to my orchestra a whole hour early.

Now I'm sitting listening to the thunderous pattering of the rain and Schwarzkopf on my gramophone, which might stand for the two elements dividing up the last few days; but I have only to lift my eyes to see my beautiful fireplace. I'm so *proud* to possess it.

November 4th

A Sunday morning, pure blue sky. I lie propped in pillows with the coffee busily dripping through my coffee-pot beside me, the Sunday papers spread on the eiderdown and a deep overwhelming sadness and sense of the pathos of everything.

I visited Phil Nichols in hospital two days ago and found him far gone in melancholia. Lionel Penrose, asked by me how to deal with such states, says, 'It doesn't make the smallest difference what you do.'

Later. Having visited Phil again I'm not sure that 'depression' is all he's suffering from. He may even be gravely ill. He was dressed and sitting up on a hard chair in his small prison room. I feel terribly sorry for him, and the extraordinarily bleak unsympathetic uncaring attitude of the nurses greatly distressed me, but I had the satisfaction of seeing him considerably brighter by the end of my visit.

I left the nursing-home glad that I'd gone, and drove off to Richmond to lunch with Anne and Heywood. Walk in Kew Gardens, through the immaculately kept rock gardens; into the crystal palace full of ferns – such ferns as I never saw before, with great brown bulbs at their hearts, green flaps like elephants' ears, long dangling fleshy hands with attenuated fingers and marvellously strong curling fronds thick in black hairs. A few children were straggling round with their parents who were trying to divert their attention from the naked private parts of the statues to the plants. However, 'What's that *lydy* doing?' a little girl asked, pointing to Apollo.

November 6th

I spent yesterday morning in close company sitting cheek-by-jowl with a young, wholesome and pretty Oxford graduate (female) going over the proof of my last Spanish translation.

In the course of this long gruelling morning's work a shattering telephone call came through from Little Barbara saying that Clive's operation this morning had been 'frightful'. It was cancer and they had removed a great deal, including bone, and he was still unconscious. And poor old Saxon died yesterday – that at least is nothing but a mercy. The release of the sick and old is a thing one must welcome and if poor Clive is to have no more tenable life than seems likely, I wish it for him too. The way out! Oh, where is it, for the old and decrepit? Could hardly face my evening's dinner-party (Eddy Sackville and the Godleys with Dicky in afterwards) but somehow screwed myself up to it. Though it was rather as if I too were some ancient matador putting on his 'suit of lights' and creeping to meet the bull. Well, I've asked Barbara to lunch today. I'm struck by the difference between having to go through one's own hour of doom and feeling pain on behalf of others. The force of the first calls on all one's powers of resistance, whereas the second produces no outlet but quavering unhappiness.

November 7th

I've just been to see Clive and read *The Times* to him for nearly an hour. His courage and self-control and on-the-spotness, in spite of a tube in his nose and another in his arm were beyond everything, and I suppose surprised me only because he is an anxious character by nature, inclined to fuss about unnecessary details beforehand – but this, as I should have realized, is very common in intelligent and sensitive people. Slightly tense and apprehensive when I arrived, I felt only waves of affection and admiration for dear Clive, as soon as I was in his presence. His consideration and tact is wonderful and he made perfectly acute comments on everything I read him.

I seem to be having a sort of cocktail party next Tuesday, which I rather dread, but it's my way of paying Boris for his glorious mosaic, and like everything else it will come and go.

November 10th

Phyllis came to see me on Sunday night and said that Lord Evans, the Queen's doctor, told her Phil couldn't possibly recover, as the whole system of blood supply to the brain was failing. She was looking tragic but very handsome.

It was an enormous relief to go to dinner with Burgo and Henrietta on Sunday night and be with the high-spirited young, whose natural ebullience carried them along so gaily. Henrietta cooked a delicious dinner; Charlotte and Peter Jenkins were there.

November 14th

I spent the afternoon of my cocktail party in perfect calm, partly organizing it, partly typing a Freudian index. I felt not the smallest anxiety about it; it went roaring along, and indeed I quite enjoyed it. And here I sit next day, feeling full of energy, and really quite puffed-up because of having got through my party 'on my head' as it seems to me. Cooking dinner for four is far more of a business. Burgo and Henrietta's mutual devotion gave me intensest pleasure. Janetta sweetly asked Boris and me back to dinner, along with Magouche, Paddy and Joan, Eddie Gathorne-Hardy. When they all charged off to yet another party at the Harrods' at midnight, I marvelled, and felt thankful I had no temptation to go. At my party everyone behaved in character: Raymond talked to me seriously about the mosaic, said he adored it – as I believe he did – but wanted me to alter the surrounding colours and the rug in front. Rosamund murmured: 'Oh – darling! What a lovely party! How brave of you and how clever!' Julia spent hours in front of my looking-glass like a deb at a ball and then delighted everyone with her conversation. Julian was most kind and helpful with pouring drinks. And so on.

November 19th

What remains in my mind most vividly from the rich stew of last weekend at Stokke is the journey back by train with Eduardo Paolozzi sitting opposite, and the glare of a bright wintry sun shining in our eyes and lying on the surrounding fields like lacquer. My first response to him when he stumped into the living-room with his impassive face and slow husky 'Hullos' all round, was a sort of amazement. Surely no-one of intelligence could have such a *changeless* expression? And at dinner that night I was cross because he accused Raymond of being 'bitchy' as a critic – the evidence being that he didn't like Peggy Ashcroft in *The Cherry Orchard*. But he's very thoughtful in his deliberate way, and our long talk in the train was interesting – largely given over to his account of what 'occupied his mind at the moment', how he liked to run his life, his attitude to wife and children, and getting away from them, and work.

December 5th

This is the second of two days when London has been in the grip of the dreaded SMOG – dense, ice-cold, choking, in some way both exciting and neurotically terrifying. Kitty West and I left a cinema at eleven last night to find the world turned to khaki-coloured opacity through which lights and strange cries came obsessionally, the small red eyes of rear-lights moved mysteriously and very slowly about, and there were people riding on the steps of cars directing the drivers. It was dramatic and rather beautiful to look at in a Yoshio Markino sort of way, had it not been for the filth one drew in at every breath – not proper sustenance for human lungs. The tall tops of my rooms are full of it, and I have been closeted in them all day, seeing no-one but Eardley who came for a drink (a face in the desert) as Mrs Ringe hasn't of course arrived. It seems slightly less bad this evening; there's no longer the sensation as if poison-gas was trying to creep in at all the cracks and I regret having been too craven to go to my orchestra.

But the thing I must write about and which has loomed far biggest for nearly a week in my mind, to be thought about lovingly and anxiously at all hours of the day, is that Burgo came to tell me last Friday that he was going to marry Henrietta. I felt instant joy. But the possibility of such happiness for him of course makes me tremble for him. Henrietta isn't quite eighteen, and I know I shan't be able to help looking nervously after their little boat as it pushes out to sea, but in any case this is something entirely good and *plus* for Burgo. The wedding is to be just before Christmas –

and I shall come up from Julia's for it.[1] I now have a stake in the world, and the only steadying thing I felt before was that I hadn't. Perhaps I might be some use to them both, and that is a troubling and moving thought.

I have been reading through some of my old diaries and am staggered by the screams of pain that come from the pages, because I feel and know – surely I can't be wrong? – that I have had an extraordinarily happy life for the most part. Is it just that unhappiness needs to find an outlet whereas happiness enfolds one like a warm rug into silence?

December 7th

The fog closed down more densely than ever last night into a thick, almost black mud-pack pressing in on us. Through it Burgo and Henrietta and the Kees came to dinner. The happiness of the two young delighted me. I feel as if an exotic flower, an orchid perhaps, had suddenly bloomed in the London fog and I shake with terror at what might happen to it. But it is a happy agitation.

Yesterday I lunched with Eardley (we have met each foggy day like explorers in the desert). Conversation about violence; it aroused my amazement that everyone shouldn't view it with the horror I feel for it. It started from the fact that Joan had been unable to stand the film of *Billy Budd*, and had to come out, and I attacked the story for violence, sentimentality and priggishness mixed. To my amazement Eardley asked on what grounds 'one could justify being against violence'. I replied with what seemed to me at the time a conclusive argument – that violence is nearly always at the expense of other people's happiness and that the appetite grows on what it feeds on. To enjoy looking at violent films and plays or promote them was to manure a plant that was bound to bear sinister fruit. But how, how can it be necessary to say anything so obvious?

Oh, the rapture of seeing a pale blue sky today, of breathing in air, not poison-gas! Eager to get out, I went to Cameo Corner to look at some bits of jewellery – topaz and garnet and coral necklaces for a possible present for Henrietta.

---

[1] I had promised to stay with her at Lambourn while Lawrence and Jenny were together.

December 8th

Rosamond rang up last night to tell me that Phil died the day before. It was no surprise, but a very severe shock. It must have been yesterday, after his death, that I tried to ring up Phyllis 'to enquire' and the number was engaged. Now, having just finished writing to Phyllis, I feel shocked anew.

More sick-bed visiting – Clive, who does not claim pity as an ailing man, but receives one with dignity and serenity, and in the evening, a very different matter, Paul Cross, who lies abed in an over-heated, over-decorated room, his skeleton form propped on pillows, his face sunken beyond belief like a Zurbaran monk's. How much he understood of what I said to him I wasn't sure.

December 14th

On the eve of setting out for three weeks' married life with Julia, I'm very well aware of the difficulties and the possible sadness.

Could Lawrence possibly think of me as an alternative life companion for Julia, I wonder – two widowed women, lifelong friends – after all, it wouldn't be so very odd. But I know that I can never live with anyone else again but myself, certainly not Julia.

December 19th

Like a piece of meat soaking in a marinade, I have for three days been lying soaking in Julia's country peace, leaving far behind the gas-ring of London life on which I have been a simmering bubbling pot. What a difference! So far the change has been purely restorative and I feel myself developing into a cow from chewing the quiet cud of this luscious pasture. It is, I realize, my first longish spell of country life since I left Ham Spray and everything is, I believe, going very well. At any rate I'm getting great enjoyment from Julia's company; she has arranged the house so that almost nothing has to be done in the way of cooking and shopping, and helping to do that little gives me a modicum of self-respect. We are looked after by dear little Mrs Rose, piping like a blackbird in the kitchen (what the Gowings call her 'tuneless whistle' but it has a charming flutelike quality), and the evening meal is usually all got ready in advance and therefore tends to be warmed-up meat, say, with warmed-up brussels sprouts and warmed-up mashed potatoes, followed by warmed-up mince pies! It suits me fine, though I'm not sure how Julia fits it into her own food faddism. We both do long hours of work (though my progress with my Spanish translation is shockingly slow) and take many brisk walks on brilliant cold mornings with blue sky, perhaps a wind and the sensational English winter gloss on leaves, red berries and twigs. Mrs Rose is to be told over Christmas that Lawrence's old aunt is desperately ill and that's why he's not coming down. She has, in fact, just most conveniently died.

The Charley's Aunt element which has always beset the Gowings' lives is here, mercifully relieving gloom. It is even more present in Julia's new 'Goblin Tea-Made', which might be something out of one of her stories. She staggered to my flat last week with three large parcels done up in Christmas wrappings, and I brought them down in my Mini. When undone they revealed a device combining alarm-clock with a kettle and hideous square teapot with the spout at one corner. Julia spent hours putting it together and brooding over the instructions anxiously and lovingly: ' "Depress platform". Now, what on earth can that mean? Oh, I suppose this is it, but it seems to be permanently depressed on one side already. I ca see it's going to be me that's depressed, n t the platform.' We then went round to someone in the village lled Maureen who had a similar machine, for enlightenment. Jul plans to be woken at six-thirty or so and do several hours' 'work' before breakfast. 'But the worst of it is, I simply *hate* tea,' she ended up surprisingly (after saying it had 'cost the earth'), 'so I plan to put Nescafé in instead.' The machine has worked and so far she is delighted with it. What goes on in her working hours, either here in her bedroom or in the London Library, is a mystery. Quite a lot of it is reading books of popular science, highbrow weeklies or articles on electronic music, from which she makes notes and derives stimulation.

December 20th

There is only one danger I have to keep a wary eye open for in conversation with Julia, and that is to avoid anything like a rational argument. This sounds more cramping than it is: there's a whole world of fascinating talk left, exploring our way through regions of cobweblike delicacy concerned with human behaviour, books, aesthetics and lots of other things. I've long known that if some matter of general principle arises about which she feels deeply but has not the equipment to argue logically, and if I get into my arguing boots (which boots I see to *her* seem more aggressive and combative than they feel to me, their wearer – who loves arguing more than almost anything) a sharp note of fear comes into her voice and she begs for the subject to be changed.

December 21st

It's probably impossible in this life of seclusion with two prime egotists sitting in the middle of a carefully-constructed nest, for tiny incidents not to bulk large. Amused as I am by them, I become irritated at times as a result of Julia's obsessional pernicketyness. Everything must be done just so and not another way, no room for improvisation – the opposite (directly) of Janetta, say. Yet though I'm sure Julia is convinced her methods are the best, just look at the difference in the meals which result! I do hope I shan't be offered 'warmed-up Spam' again. I can hardly swallow it, and was staggered when offered some in my sandwich lunch for today: 'A Spam sandwich might be rather nice?' Might it, indeed! The exact ritual also has to be preserved concerning the coffee-pot, the stove, the amount of air let into rooms, the turning-off of electricity. The water in the coffee-pot must go to within half an inch of the top *exactly*! The coffee must be ground 105 revolutions *exactly*! When I started to pour myself some coffee before it had all dripped through, Julia rushed in to say I mustn't do it because it would alter the *exact* proportions she had arranged. But this morning came an Aunty-Loo[1]-like cry from the ash-bucket outside the garden door: 'AH! now I'm afraid it's not a very good idea to put paper in the bucket – only ashes – in case it catches alight.'
. . . Needless to say, I hadn't been near the bucket; these were the residues left by the 'men' who had been putting anti-burglar screws on the windows. This house is full of precautions against every contingency. Having said all the above, I really must add that stifled but hilarious amusement makes up for the bulk of my response to it, and irritation is a minute seed and has all been exorcized by setting it down.

[1] Alys Russell, first wife of Bertrand Russell, brought Julia up.

138

December 23rd

Burgo is a married man. Everything about the wedding was to me deeply touching and charming and it has left me in a state close to anguish. I hadn't expected that I would hardly get to sleep last night for the passionate longing I felt for Burgo and Henrietta's happiness. Burgo's confidence and assurance over the wedding arrangements amazed me. Everything was splendidly organized and they had done it all themselves – lobster mayonnaise, and a fruit flan made by Henrietta herself as she hung her head bluebell-wise with modesty to admit. I think they both enjoyed the whole thing to the full and so did we all – Bunny, Duncan, Angelica, Amaryllis and David Gillies, the best man.

Notes on the wedding: the absolute charm of Duncan, arriving with a button-hole in a white paper bag, beaming at everyone. The geniality of Bunny, who suddenly began talking about the necessity of leaving one's body to the doctors with a look of great jollity on his face (more suitable to the occasion than the subject). His father's mistress, old Nellie someone-or-other, has just died and when Bunny went to arrange the funeral he found to his relief that the body-snatchers had already been, and all trouble and expense were spared him. 'You just ring up the Ministry of Offal, Sackville Street,' is what I remember him saying, but I suppose he can't have.

December 26th

I am living in a dungeon whose walls are made out of the intense cold, within which Julia's and my dark and secluded existence is enclosed. Here I sit all day in this dark sunless house – the room in which I spend my day is like a Spanish 'interior' room looking on to the frozen courtyard where sparrows and starlings noisily quarrel over scraps of bread. I feel as if Julia and I were serving a prison sentence. For what crime? Or to what end? She, I suppose, gets the satisfaction of believing she's toiling towards an artistic achievement, but I can't feel anything like that about my trans-lation – merely that it's an activity I enjoy, and which will bring me in some money – for what? To *live*. In brief, I hardly feel human here, though I greatly enjoy Julia's company, and am like a schoolchild counting the days to my return to West Halkin Street.

December 27th

Claustrophobic, soft and white, the snow is falling steadily, and lies already inches deep in the garden where the birds quarrel noisily over their crusts. Julia and I have been out for a walk along the slippery roads, dressed more or less as scarecrows, Julia holding an umbrella only part of which would go up, and wearing an immense mac over quantities of jerseys and coats. Twice she fell suddenly full length, noiselessly into the snow. Cars slither and slide around corners, stable-boys go by on spindly bow-legs or greet one from bicycles. Last night we had a delightful visit from Janetta, and Jaime. What excuse for Lawrence's absence did Julia give to Janetta? She certainly told the Carringtons that Lawrence's Aunt Edith was gravely ill. But some people have been told he's abroad on Gulbenkian business. Some, I fancy, have had a story combining both elements and, between the two, poor Julia is completely bewildered. I heard her muttering to herself: 'That's it, I think Aunt Edith had better die today.'

December 28th

The pall of snow still shrouds us, so the prison sentence goes on, and contacts with the outside world have been barred by the snow. A very slight thaw but the snow is still thick, and walking up the road towards the Carringtons I was dazzled by the virginal beauty of the Pollock theatre[1] trees, smooth fields, and in back gardens the lovely sight of wheels, tubs and farm tools each with its thick white coat. The sky had turned a pale apricot and the furthest slope of the hill was an iced wedding-cake faintly blushed with palest rose against the baby-blue sky.

I've thought a lot lately, with more detachment and even pleasure than I've been able to before, about my life with Ralph. It would be terrible if, in the process of growing scar tissue, I should lose the completely focussed sharpness of remembering the details of

---

[1] A toy theatre of traditional design.

our happiness together, of our tremendous jokes and laughter and of the life-bringing current of his love.

December 29th

C'est le dernier pas qui coûte. Some cross remark shouted up at me by Julia about the sitting-room cosy stove suddenly let loose all my indignation at being spoken to twenty times a day as if I were a half-witted kitchen-maid whom she was hoping to train but despairing of, instead of an elderly highbrow. I lay therefore in bed, fulminating against this pressure of her bourgeois, cautious life-style and every fibre in me that believes in spontaneity and freedom and bohemian improvisation was in revolt. The irony of it is that she is the only one who has seriously mismanaged the stove and jolly nearly burnt the whole thing out one night.

Oh, well, there's nothing to be done but stick it out somehow. I toyed with ideas of saying I couldn't bear it and must go back to London, but it would be too cruel, situated as she is. To add to the general horror, yesterday a bitter wind arose and howled round the house and much more snow has fallen and looks like falling. The Kees were due to come to dinner tonight but it will obviously be impossible, and I would have welcomed a diversion.

1963

January 1st: Lambourn

But how is it possible to believe that we have crossed into a new year when the same deep eiderdown of whiteness lies feet deep over everything and more, *more* snow is falling from the sky. I lay awake last night listening to the Lambourn church bells dismally tolling for a full hour the death and birth of the years. Afterwards the blessed silence was broken by the wild yells of Lambourn stable-lads.

January 2nd

Telephone call from the Carringtons, who are worried about Joanna, snowed up at Buttermere. Julia was struck because they said, 'We thought you'd like to know we were all right.' 'I see we ought to have been *worrying* about them!' Julia said to me in surprise and this led to a lunch conversation wherein I'm afraid I trod badly on her spiritual corns. I said something about the importance of friends being brought home to one by the snow, and that it was odd to find ourselves so nipped by the fight against the cold that we almost lost the desire for communication with them. Then Julia said that she 'hadn't time for friends in her life' and I (voicing a long buried secretion of irritation) replied that if I didn't value friendships I should shoot myself. Julia turned rather pink and declared that a creative writer with no servant had no time for anything else. I said that it seemed to me she *had* a splendid servant and also that I thought most creative artists and writers did have something to spare for friendship. The highest names were used as examples – Henry James, Flaubert, Turgenev, Charlie Chaplin – but oh! what a mistake it all was, and I was much to blame for driving her thus into a corner with some of her own assumptions, which are pretty neurotic. The fire catches the wisps of dry hay before one can stop it. Afterwards Julia generously came and apologized for 'having lost her wool', saying that she could only put it down to 'having some of Oliver and Marjorie's genes in her'.[1] After this all was smooth and serene.

January 3rd, Thursday

Yesterday's snow seemed to amplify the sounds of the squabbling birds, of the cold winds rattling the frozen bushes, of Julia clearing her throat upstairs, and Mrs Rose's 'tuneless whistle' in the kitchen. Meanwhile the approach of a new blizzard was reported at intervals all day in sinister tones by B.B.C. announcers. At lunch yesterday Julia suddenly suggested that we should cut and run before it struck; and as soon as lunch was over I went to make enquiries of the garage about the state of the Newbury road (thirteen miles), the running of buses and possibility of hiring a car. 'You'd be safest in a bus *if* you can get one,' was the reply. 'Otherwise we never know, and with this blizzard we can't never know if the men'll get through with them.' So, crestfallen, I reported all this to Julia, who is panicky beyond anyone I've ever met.

January 6th, Sunday: West Halkin Street

We're out. I got to London yesterday and am on the whole immensely glad to be here.

The 'great blizzard' turned out rather a flop, though it did lay down another three inches of snow and some drifts. Then, two days ago, a slight thaw began and sun came out, and hearing that people were 'getting through' to Newbury I began to hanker to go in my Mini if it were humanly possible, and to say to myself: 'If other people can get through, why shouldn't I?' So I took a spade and hacked out a path through the somewhat softened three-foot-deep drift outside the garage door, behind which Mini had been so long imprisoned, having done which I felt triumphant and a great load of claustrophobia lifted. I asked Julia if she wouldn't come with me. After only a moment's pause she said she would

---

[1] Julia's father and aunt.

be so nervous that perhaps it was better to go by jeep from the garage, and train. From this decision flowed calm and amiability, though there wasn't a moment from then till midnight when she wasn't making preparations for every emergency in minutest detail. She says she's always done this, even when young.

I really enjoyed the freedom and adventure for Mini and me in getting out. The road to Newbury was slushy and narrow between high banks of beaten snow: after that it was plain sailing, and I got to Halkin Street (with what a sensation of escape!) just in time to buy whiskey and bacon before the shops shut.

So here I am hard at work straightening out my material life. Saw the Campbells yesterday, and Janetta and her family.

January 10th

Burgo and Henrietta gave a wedding party two nights ago which was an unqualified success.

January 17th

I have woken early after a short uneasy night. More snow has fallen, but stopped in time for me to go to the first orchestra practice last night – a flattish affair; I was the only second violin there. 'Flattish' – that is now my life. I've truckled under to it, accepted it, and recognize that the acuteness of my unhappiness is blunted, but I subsist in a foggy and depressing landscape, lit by very few flares of excitement, or interest. A strike – or rather unofficial go-slow – of electricians at this time of grizzly cold raises the usual unsolved problem as to whether striking is to be condemned as a form of force. I think it is, although I would so much rather agree with Frances Phipps[1] (whose voice comes over the telephone from snow-bound Pewsey full of indignation against those who not only condemn the electricians but also enjoy hating them). A spinster lady from the First Violins last night poured out a torrent of this very hate, saying that the electricians were as 'wicked as the Germans, putting up men, women and children and shooting them'. The only person I've really discussed this strike

---

[1] Widow of Sir Eric Phipps, Ambassador at Paris, and a recent very left-wing friend.

with is Mrs Ringe, and staunch Labour woman as she is, her Scotch common-sense puts her against the strikers.

January 21st

Eardley, the Cochemés and the Penroses all dined here last night and we had (I thought) a delightful evening with interesting and lively talk, ranging part of the time into scientific territory – sympathetic ground for both Cochemé[1] and Lionel; and Lionel in his diffident offhand way delighted us all by describing experiments now being made to enclose a fertilized human ovum in a rabbit's uterus – 'or perhaps a cow's', he added – 'to produce two tiny people'. There was talk also of giants. He told us about a woman he'd been to see in Ireland who had given birth to five children each weighing from thirteen to fifteen pounds at birth, and finally one of eighteen pounds. At three they were like children of ten. When adult they were of normal size and splendid healthy specimens. Eardley told the extraordinary story of the canaries which apparently sing elaborate tunes dating from the eighteenth century, and having been handed down from canary to canary.

February 1st

We begin February with a new waft of snow, biting cold winds, and slippery pavements. It is more somehow than one 'bargained' for. It has driven me back into the socket of my own resources as a sledgehammer drives a stake into soft earth, and I have an uneasy feeling that the pressure put on those resources is pounding them into grey powdery ash. I have 'come to terms' in some sort of way with my life, but the strangeness of that life sometimes makes my heart almost stand still. It consists above all in just driving myself forcibly along from one activity or passive employment to the next, never leaving a gap. And never *really* asking myself for what, why this effort has to be undertaken, because I know it's for nothing. That's what a life without love is – nothing.

---

[1] Jacques, Joan's husband, biologist and meteorologist.

February 9th

I think a lot about marriage, and the astonishing effect of clamping together two personalities, who however deeply loving and mutually appreciative, have each a separate core – not perhaps incommunicable but almost unalterable. Ralph was a very strong character and the disappearance of that constant source of interest, vitality, amusement and sometimes irritation has left me a thin grey husk. I particularly miss the rogue elephant side of his character which gave me so much delight and made me laugh so often.

February 16th

To Crichel yesterday afternoon, for about five days. I had been looking forward to it, but was it just another stuffed carrot to drive myself along, poor deluded old donkey, from day to day? I've been given Eddy's[1] room. I've slept here before and find that the powerful aroma of his personality stifles me as the impersonal one of the spare room does not. Its feminine side is expressed in literally hundreds of tiny knicknacks ranged all round the room, little white china pieces, Victorian shell-decorations, enamel boxes, even jewels: and then beside me hangs the Ivory Christ with a praying chair in front of it and a rosary, which affects me unpleasantly. Why is it not more neutral? Why not think of it as a mere *object*, perhaps even quite beautiful? But I can't; it's swathed and clouded with emotional debris.

February 17th

Good resolutions worked rather well yesterday and I did a lot of work, which was what I wanted. Raymond too disappears all morning to work or snooze and then lies on his back on the sofa, head well below his knees. Desmond and I listened to most of Monteverdi's *Incorazione di Poppea*. Canasta in the evening, a lot of talk about the use of words, the sexual morals of the young, and the way we are being poisoned by chemical manures.

---

[1] Sackville-West, Lord Sackville.

February 20th

I'm very happy with Desmond nowadays. He is like an optimistic, constantly evolving Handelian tune. Yesterday he left after an early lunch and I was left alone with Raymond, when we had rather a good talk about the technique of living. He has told me a lot about his African tour and I think I've questioned and taken an interest as much as he could wish, following each hare that started from the grass in its dash over the fields, but I don't think (oddly enough) he's as much at ease with me as am I with him. I was eager to put on my frog feet and plunge into greater profundities – namely to discuss an article by Kenneth Clark on Modern Art which Raymond had given me to read. It set forth a curiously inconclusive theory – he calls it the Blot and the Diagram – but it surely isn't very different to Form and Content? Anyway, it's thought-provoking but I found not for the first time that Raymond doesn't really like 'going into' things, and when I asked him what he felt about it he said vaguely: 'Oh, I don't know. I just thought it very brilliant.'

After dinner he began to talk a little sadly about his writing, saying that he was afraid he didn't give the *Sunday Times* what they want. Before I went up to bed he complained of 'waffling' books on ideas by people unqualified to evolve them (he was reviewing two), and I remarked how odd it was for them to like thinking if they couldn't do it, as it was the most difficult thing in the world. Raymond said, 'I know. I can't do it, and I never try.' In fact there hangs about him a rather sad unconfident air as well as that final and central area of reserve, which I would have liked to approach if not to penetrate, even if only because it seems to be a cold and lonely place.

February 24th: London

A visit from Julia yesterday, wrapped to the eyes in furs, scarves and flannel petticoats. Returning Gerald's last book which I had lent her, she launched an attack on Gerald and Ralph (I think now it was chiefly Ralph she was aiming at): 'I was deeply shocked to find they actually *enjoyed* the War.' I was amazed by the naiveté of her thinking that young men of nineteen could have been pacifists while they were actually engaged in a war. For she looked back with the innocence of her curiously unfurnished sixty-year-old mind at this other world of young tough men, and (as usual) judged. She also talked a lot about her own neurotic character, and said several times, 'I can't live alone'. What is my responsibility towards her, as her oldest friend? I am selfishly wondering, and so far my answer is: I'll do everything I possibly can, short of giving up my independent solitary life. She asked me about myself and how I found living alone and I was able to answer quite truthfully that I found it the only possible alternative to living with Ralph.

A delightful evening, going with Desmond, Eardley and Pansy Lamb[1] (after dining here) to a concert at the Italian Institute in Belgrave Square, given by some madrigal singers. We were in the front row looking at these six intensely Italian figures sitting round a dining-room table. At one end the chief soprano sat with her vast plump bosom and arms rising from her evening dress, rolling her beautifully socketed Italianate eyes with an infinitely comic, charming and coy expression towards the plump baritone at the other end, who with curvilinear gestures of hands covered in gold rings and gold bracelets was conducting the proceedings. An oval-faced counter-tenor looking like the young Marcel Proust delighted us all with the way he threw up his head and contributed his *miaow miaow*'s to that famous chorus, and the bass was a handsome Roman-looking brunetto with sculptured hair. The music was lovely, and gay too except for the heavenly but sad Monteverdi *Lasciate mi morire*. It made me 'climb up two rungs of the ladder' of well-being. The whole atmosphere of the concert, including the Italian faces amongst the audience has switched my mind towards the beckoning charms of Italy.

February 25th

After a musical mid-day with the Penroses I came back and spent the rest of the day – some seven hours of it – in solitude here and most of it in powerful blotting-paper-like absorption of what was given out by my excellent wireless. It was all of interest: but especially an hour's programme in French about Proust by people who had known him, ending with a long and extraordinarily touching account of his deathbed by Celeste (the Françoise of *A la*

---

[1] Widow of Henry Lamb, painter.

recherche), in which her emotion came through in the purest, sincerest way, so that when she broke down and sobbed every listener must surely have done the same. Here was reality doing something art hardly ever can and causing an emotion I find it hard to differentiate from that (say) of the last act of Verdi's *Otello*. A direct commentary on life; something which though so infinitely sad had a cathartic effect because of its flawless certainty of touch. Had it been a work of art one would have guessed there must be some formal qualities to make it so inspiring. But obviously there were not: she was just remembering intensely, groping back through the past, under colour of the strongest possible emotion, to something that was of supreme tragic importance to her. Then what exactly turns a response to life into a work of art? And is it possible to create a work of art unconsciously by the sincerity of response?

March 1st

Musically speaking, I have been hovering between two stools. Vaguely discontented with my Hampstead orchestra, I eagerly hurried off yesterday to try another, a Medical one heard of from the Penroses. The first two sessions were alarming, a *much* higher standard, a conductor with a difficult beat, a programme they had already been practising for some weeks. Then, at the third go last night, the authentic magic caught on. What had seemed almost out of reach was suddenly attainable with an effort, and the excitement of becoming integrated into this huge mass of combined sound set a match to the sticks that had been waiting unlit, or at most giving out a little greasy smoke. It is a much bigger, more professional affair, very much alive, and composed of intelligent interesting faces, old and young, white and black, including a lot of German and Austrian Jews. Our concert has Hepzibah Menuhin for a soloist. The excitement, the lift and intoxication with which I flew home down the Edgware Road last night has proved to me this is what I want, and though it's difficult for me, I now *think* (with hard work) I can perhaps make the grade.

Ever since Burgo's wedding, Bunny's remark about the convenience and simplicity of leaving one's body to a hospital has been rumbling in my mind and finally I took action on it. Two days ago I found myself staring in bewilderment at an envelope with 'INSPECTOR OF ANATOMY' written on it in large black letters. I thought for a moment I'd gone mad. But no, this is the gentleman who arranges for the hospitals' corpse-supply. I must admit it gave me a slight *frisson* as I saw myself laid out cold and stiff and pale, or kept on ice for two years, which seems possible. I shoved it away with a little burst of escapism. Then yesterday, 'This won't do,' I thought, and fished it out and dealt with it. I rang up H.M. Inspector. A delightful humorous Scotch voice answered, recommending me to leave myself to 'the nearest medical school' – because 'ye might die up in the north country or somewhere'. So it's done now and I feel another cupboard has been tidied.

March 3rd

Yesterday, for the first time for some while, my direct pleasure in my surroundings produced the conviction that the 'stuff' of which the visible world was made was both beautiful and exciting. It was like the return of the sense of taste after influenza. Pale but distinct, there it was, the pure but hazy blue of the sky, the cream stucco of Belgravia house-fronts, the faint brownness at the end of twigs, the sharp fresh smell of earth, wood, spring perhaps in the air, the sound of gentle hopeful twittering. It's as if a helpful person had given me an arm and hoisted me up a step, just as my contact with my new orchestra did on Wednesday.

March 7th

The cloudless blue days follow each other and my pleasure in them goes on, though I feel suspicious of it and view it askance.

Last night I dined in a new world, with Nicko and Mary Henderson. Arthur Koestler was there; I'd not seen him since Alpbach, and his first remark to me was, 'Are you still against religion?' 'Oh yes,' I said. He looked inclined to take this up and pursue it, and at some point I said I was a hardened rationalist or something to that effect. He looked cross: 'It is out of fashion now.' I laughed – provokingly, I dare say – and said, 'I don't care a pin for fashion.' 'No. Nor do I,' he said quickly, but more crossly still, and then with a lecturing expression: 'There is no longer a basis for rejecting religion.' There's no means of discussing ideas with Koestler, as Ralph long ago found out. You can either listen to him haranguing or not. He won't listen to you. I don't think the better of him for that, clever man though he undoubtedly is.

The 'lower classes' and death: Mrs Ringe's husband has been sufficiently ill lately for him to be taken to hospital. In talking to me she makes no bones about the trouble he is, how irritable and hard to please, how he 'won't pull himself together and try to do things', yet she's not blind to how ill he is. At the same time she refers often to the possibility of his death, pensions, and whether she should ever marry again. I'm sure she thinks constantly and simply about all that. She says nothing 'in bad taste' yet it gives me a shock that anyone should be able to contemplate their nearest and dearest as alive and dead at one and the same time. I almost long to beg her to be kinder to him and try to put herself in the state of mind of a sinking, dying man, and realize the horror of it for him. But I suppose she is being much more realistic than I was for instance, who could only accept the possibility of death when it was forced on me and for short gasping stretches at a time, to build up as quickly as possible an optimistic ostrichism. Yet I consider myself a realist and my education ought to have trained me to face facts and control my thoughts, and not slide off into clichés like 'It's only the thought,' or 'We've all got it coming to us,' or 'It'll all come out in the wash.'

March 12th: Stokke, a large party

Walked along the canal with Magouche on a wild and showery afternoon. It was beautiful in spite of the stormy weather, with the canal's grey waters covered in quite big waves over which the swans tossed with ruffled feathers and proudly curving heads; the pale biscuit-coloured reeds behind. I went another walk through the forest with Robin Fedden;[1] all around us we saw exquisite springlike glossiness, snowdrops, woods tender and furry-looking in the distance, life-giving flashes of sun.

I had my usual moments of profound loneliness and withdrawal to my room, tired of always being the oldest, and feeling that Dee Ayer[2] in particular resented what she would think of, as Koestler did, as my old-fashioned outlook. I clambered back painfully onto

[1] Writer and alpinist.
[2] Wife of A.J. (Freddie) Ayer, the philosopher.

the perch of my identity, but had moments of pitiful longing for my sad but only little *home*.

Should I or shouldn't I go to Ham Spray?

I did go. But OH. And I think now I'll never go again.

March 14th: London

Spirits low yesterday. Julia was disapproving and snubbing on the telephone as only she can be, telling me I led a 'whirl' of a life, 'telephone ringing all day', 'arrangements squeezed in with difficulty'. When I said this had no resemblance to the truth she said with finality: 'Oh, yes: Lawrence noticed it too.' She went on to say that she wasn't feeling well enough to go out or see people, only to work. And thus I was put securely in my place. I feel a little hurt, I suppose. She has herself experienced the difficulties of living alone and found them so crushing that she told me she would do anything in the world rather than face them again. My solution is different from hers. I couldn't possibly live *except* alone, but I deal with my problem in my own way by seeing people every day, and throwing myself as much as possible into their lives.

Yesterday I lunched with Eardley and Mattei at a Greek restaurant, and was unspeakably lowered in spirits by Oxford Street in the rain. If one wants to keep afloat, *never go near Oxford Street*, it is too crushing a view of the human race. That's what London seemed like when I came to it from Ham Spray, and that's what I believe all of it will one day become.

I even sat down and started writing Julia a letter of justification of my mode of life – but oh God, what's the use?

March 15th, Friday

Today is my 63rd birthday, so I've just remembered, and perhaps that's why such an all-pervading, soggy but also fluttery and fevered gloom settled on me from the moment of waking. I take my surgeon's scalpel and plunge it into the living tissue in the hopes either of finding the tumour or letting out some of the poison.

Loneliness has been accentuated by Julia's 'writing me off' (so it seemed to me) the other day, as a futile member of the rat-race unworthy to mix with serious people like her and Lawrence. Of course I'm exaggerating this quite deliberately, just as one feels a sore place to see how much it hurts. I've thought a lot about our lifelong friendship and wondered how much rivalry there is in it – on either side – and how much I am over-critical of her. Why isn't it easier just to appreciate people for what they are – as dear old Bunny does for instance – rather than dissect them so remorselessly? I am in a mood at the moment to take the guilt for most things on myself and perhaps I can turn such a whipping-bout to good account and resolve to be better.

My work is one source of anxiety. *The President*[1] is finished and now being typed. I'm very dissatisfied with it indeed. The publishers think it's an 'important book'. I have been so embedded for months past in the appalling difficulties of the task that I have hardly any notion how it will read. Ralph thought I was a good translator, and I had confidence in myself – now suddenly I've lost it all and am full of anxieties. And this translating has been such a source of security and happiness to me in the past; I hate to think of giving it up. Part of this uneasiness comes from my dread of stepping out into the unknown with no banister to lean upon in the shape of a daily task. How to meet the emergency, what reserves to call on? It's always the same: courage, courage, courage, a realistic and rational attitude to the problem.

In the evening to my Medical orchestra and afterwards to a party at the Royal Academy given by Edward Le Bas in honour of his collection of pictures which are on show there. I couldn't see the pictures properly, but the *people* were strikingly interesting to look at; and of course there were many, many old friends – Cochemés, Macfarlanes, Raymond, Bunny and Angelica, Duncan, Burgo and Henrietta and heaven knows who besides.

March 16th

Went across the Square to the Italian Institute to hear the Italian String Quartet. I was unmoved by them and couldn't decide why – too smooth and swoopy? A lack of brilliance, bite, dynamics? A sort of mayonnaise consistency? As a spectacle, however, they are

---

[1] A translation of the major work of Miguel Asturias, Guatemalan Nobel Prize winner.

quite extraordinary. With their music almost at ground level, they bent and swooned like four dervishes above it – all but the 'cellist who maintained a rocklike stability. The second violin, the only woman, behaved in a distractingly theatrical manner, bending almost double at times or rolling her eyes to high heaven and parting her lips in a sort of musical orgasm, while her finely-drawn eyebrows moved up and down regularly in time to the beat. A kind little old lady next to me, an ex-violinist, with her clasped hands trembling all the time in a sort of palsy, talked to me in the intervals, and I felt grateful for her friendliness.

March 21st

I am always happy with the Cecils at Oxford. With both Rachel and David I feel in a spontaneous and sympathetic accord which is no way an effort. It is life, not just existence. Impossible to remember the content of all our lively conversations, except for one on Saturday night when Hugh and Emma Cavendish[1] (both facing their history finals) talked entertainingly about their feelings about their work. Heavens, what a business to stuff oneself with accurately remembered facts and somehow or other manage to retain them till the time comes to relax the sphincters of the brain and let them out onto the examination sheets. Both were philo-sophical in their different ways of dealing with anxiety: Hugh quite simply reflected that it would be worse if he were going to be shot. Emma thought it was foolish to waste her last months at Oxford *dis*enjoying herself, so she had embarked on a piece of fascinating research on Byzantium, quite useless from the exam point of view. Rachel and David are *happy*, I believe, and that's so rare that it's a great credit to them. They have worked hard to achieve it and, incidentally, give happiness to many others (such as me).

Spring in North Oxford is hideous and touching, like a very ugly young girl in exquisitely pretty clothes. Fat buds on lilac bushes, crocuses in every back garden, a few snowdrops still, and mud – that scrumptious under-estimated substance. I walked alone past the back of Summerfields. The little boys were running about the playing-fields kicking footballs and making a united, high, sustained, barbarous noise ('*waa-waa-waa*'). A few deeper voices,

[1] The Devonshires' elder daughter.

responsible in tone, of prefects could be heard pompously giving instructions to lesser fry. But they were all caught fast in the machine like flies in fly-paper. Then, at the remotest corner of the grounds, as far as they could get from the heart of school life I came across a happy little group, rosy-cheeked and absorbed, making a glorious 'place' out of old bricks, moss and leaves. Sympathetic nonconformists!

March 23rd: London

Last night I went with Eardley to hear Dadie[1] speak on Shakespeare and Troy at the Royal Institution – very, very fascinating. The lecture room is a steep circular bank of seats – so steep as to be very uncomfortable – and these were filled with distinguished-looking, highly intelligent and elderly faces. At the centre and bottom of the amphitheatre stood the lecturer's desk under a strong light, and exactly as the clock struck nine Dadie rushed impetuously in, bent over the desk, leaning both hands on it and launched forth without an instant's pause into a lively torrent of words, the beginning of his discourse. It was really admirable. He read his quotations in a voice of intense vitality and emotion, leaving me convinced that Elizabethan literature was a dazzlingly exciting, tremendously inspiring affair. Nothing of the don, nothing arid about him – just this splendid, infectious enthusiasm.

April 2nd

A page has been turned and fallen back with a loud flap – I have handed *The President* in to Gollancz and no more can be done to it. The last week before its final launching into Henrietta Street was quite fantastically hectic, my 'emotional little' typist having let me down at the last moment. I got an agency to take it on but my luck was out: the last parcel of typescript disappeared in the post and I began to feel the physical universe was against me. However, a delightful postman telephoned me to say he had just opened a bag and found it, so I dashed off in trusty Mini and picked it up somewhere near Clapham Junction! Arriving at West Halkin Street after the weekend I found a telephone message to

[1] George Rylands.

say that Mr Hilary Rubinstein would especially like to see me when I brought in the last chapters.

My heart sank. So this was it: I had been summoned to the headmaster's study. 'No, Partridge minor,' he would say, 'this work simply isn't good enough. You must do it all again.' Or, 'We'll have to scrap it,' or something. Off I went to face my Waterloo. Then my astonished ears heard a jolly Mr Rubinstein say that Mr Gollancz had read all the first part and thought it splendid and was delighted with my translation. Shortly afterwards the great man himself blew in, haloed by his fluffy grey hair, hand outstretched and said: 'I *congratulate* you. Your translation is really excellent!'

The shock was almost too great. What must a condemned prisoner feel when they bring a last-minute reprieve? Flatness I suspect, and so did I. I still do, though I know that somewhere beneath it lies an immense relief.

April 3rd

The relief of my visit to Gollancz is beginning to wear off and the usual hedge of prickly-pear *angst* sprouts up once more with its question-thorns – what? when? which? why? I went last night to a birthday-party given by Julian in Janetta's back room and didn't much enjoy it.

Such parties are not for me; the fragments of conversation one is able to snatch here and there are pointless. What is left over from it all? Nothing.

April 10th

Frances Phipps came to lunch, bringing me an envelope with 'Frances to Frances' written on it – her manifesto, she calls it, about the nuclear threat and her 'hatred of hate' and the Cold War. She thinks partly with her heart instead of her mind and this has both advantages and drawbacks. Her instincts are entirely good but she doesn't know what to do about them. Her 'manifesto' was rather touching. She wanted to keep herself up to the mark of minding the nuclear horror – as if she were in any danger of not minding it! She wanted to *do* something to express her feelings also, but could think of nothing better than writing BAN THE

BOMB on her little motor-car. She had also laid out various principles for action – the chief one I disagreed with was 'Don't argue', for that is almost the only action I think worth taking, though I agree with her that an argument is useless if one gets angry. The only hope is to argue *mildly*, and with diabolical ingenuity if need be to fit one's adversary. I suppose I don't feel nearly as guilty as she does for doing so little to further what I so passionately believe in because I'm more pessimistic and fatalistic, but I realized as I talked to her that I do set great store by testifying to my beliefs and also not allowing the implication that they are other than they are to stand unchallenged. This is what I would like to aim at, but the testimony should always be reasonable and quiet. If in doubt, stop and think before you speak. Then don't be afraid to say what you believe. These would be the maxims of my 'manifesto'.

Last night I had a 'major experience', going to *Don Carlos* with Eddy Sackville. It was a splendid performance – with Gobbi, Christoff and the negress Grace Bumbry. The audience was wildly enthusiastic, the performers melted visibly in their fire. When the negress got her greatest ovation, tears filled her eyes and I saw her brown lips repeating 'Thank you, thank you, thank you,' over and over again. And what a magnificent opera it is!

April 13th: Good Friday

Alone in my flat after packing my bags for Skye; I am taking no work of any description, and feel like someone who for the first time tries to walk without a stick after having broken their leg.

Oh these departures! I find them heartbreakingly lonely. Much as a soldier gulps his rum ration before an attack, I look forward to the peg of whiskey I shall soon be swallowing.

April 16th

Lying in bed in Skye (my breakfast eaten), from where I see the familiar but matchless view, silver and mist-swathed where yesterday afternoon it was blue and brilliant. With Colin and Clodagh I have had three days touring through marvellously beautiful country, and however vividly I seemed to remember the peculiar fascination of this crystal-clear yet varied landscape it has once more astounded me. There's nowhere to equal it, except parts of the

157

West of Ireland – not France, Spain or even Greece. Why then did I wake in such deep sadness at five this morning and lie awake for a couple of hours turning my dismal thoughts to the futile mawkishness of Charlotte Yonge – how can the addicts think so much of her? It's servants' hall literature, totally unreal.

To go back: I met Colin and Pin at Edinburgh and by twelve the long car was packed with luggage, coats, Wuti the Pekinese with his casserole of cooked rabbit, and boxes of plants for the Skye garden. We set off across the Forth ferry and northwards past hills covered in zebra stripes of snow to Pitlochry. First night there for the opening of the Drama Festival, at which Colin was honoured guest as representative of the Arts Council. It's a bleak grey town in a confluence of valleys, and all hotels were full to bursting. Colin went to one, while Pin, Wuti and I shared a tiny icy twin-bedded, 'dinky' room in a brand-new private hotel.

Later I sat in the lounge with a book, by the roaring coal fire, and once again sank happily beneath the greedy waves of sleep, left unsatisfied by my night journey, rising now and again to hear Scotch voices booming through – then there was no sound but Scotch snores.

On Easter Sunday we crossed the whole of Scotland from the dour unfriendly east to the smiling west. Colin said Glen Torridon was one of the wildest and most beautiful places in all the West Highlands; and so it was. After a bare brown stretch of moorland the sea loch opened out, and I had the sensation of filling slowly and then brimming over with delight in what I saw, and longed to take possession of some of the remote villages of one-storey cabins by the edge of the sea, by coming and staying in them for a fortnight.

We arrived at our hotel at Gairloch at about six o'clock on a still golden evening which I hope I shall never forget. It stood at the edge of the sea looking out across at far islands and promontories like velvet-covered alligators. Moss-grown rocks on one side, on the other a little church and a group of trees, every detail of their lichen-covered trunks clear in the crystalline light. Below, the sea lapped gently in over a sandy beach, so very gently that none of the shells was broken and all lay in perfect but fragile butterflies with wings expanded. I sat there for a long time, till 7 p.m. – and it was as warm as a summer evening – watching two oystercatchers paddling ecstatically in the water's edge or shutting my eyes and feeling the warm sun on my face.

Salmon for dinner and to sleep hearing the quiet sound of the sea.

April 15th: Monday

More natural beauty – a *flood* of it. Awoke to a morning as clear and brilliant, though more impermanent-seeming than last night. We started early to see Inverewe, a famous garden further north-east. It wasn't so much the flowers, lovely and surprisingly varied as they were, as the marvellous vision of sheets of water – stretches of ink, of silver, tin or copper sulphate, laid out between the snow-topped mountains. And this we went on enjoying all day long, always changing, satisfying but never cloying and perhaps never better than what I see from my bedroom window here at Kyle House. The evening of our arrival was perfectly still, golden and mellow. There were the retainers, Jackie the gardener and his wife, the other little Pekinese dog, and the garden to be quickly inspected and see what had come out since Colin and Clodagh were last here.

Do I dare turn my inner eye away from all this and look back at West Halkin Street? Will it shrivel, look false, hollow and tawdry? Well yes, it does a bit, poor little place. And how about noisy, clattering, restless, stinking old London? It seems almost insane to live in such a place, thought of from here. It's the *animals* one is drawn to in a large town, and though man is one, I can't help thinking he is at his best among the vegetables, as here, rather than surrounded by the bellowing, braying herd of his fellows. But the great advantage of nature-worship is that it draws one out of mere personal assessment and preoccupation and self-questionings such as 'What is my life like? Is it as good as I could make it?' and sinks one in a vast health-giving bath. When I remember my last visit eighteen months ago, I know I am now less poignantly unhappy and certainly less restless.

April 18th: Thursday

I have been putting out rapid temporary roots, with the eagerness born of my own native rootlessness, into the earth which sustains me at present, and greedily drawing-up impressions. Colin and Clodagh lead a life of happiness dedicated to the cultivation of their garden. They love every twig and leaf, and the worst pain they are subject to is that some twig or leaf may be burnt by frost or broken by a rough dog. I'm struck by the innocence of them both – Clodagh's smooth pink and white skin and rounded neck are those of a girl. Her kindness and equanimity and serenity are astonishing. Colin's innocence is apparent in his wide-open, bright eyes; when he wears his funny little squashy tweed gardening hat they look out from under its brim with the hopeful and touching expression of a baby under its bonnet.

Of the two Pekinese: Wuti, an elderly gentleman, is the best loved by me as well as the Mackenzies. He has the look of a Chinese sage, an immense head with a softly-domed top and his features inscribed in black like a Chinese character. Slightly uneasy intelligence looks out from his large eyes. On the journey he behaved with admirable restraint though obvious anxiety, and only once felt himself abandoned in the hotel bedroom and gave way to sudden 'hysterics'. I respect and appreciate him very much.

Suey is frivolous and feminine to a degree. Very well bred, with a black face so squashed that it's almost a hollow, she is pretty and fluffy, childishly gay and skittish (though the equivalent of forty) and loves a series of toys. The one thing she longs for is to be played with and to gain this end she bounces about, revolves like a kitten after her own tail, and as a last resort climbs up and gives a piercing monkey-like yelp!

April 20th, Saturday

Yesterday was the most brilliant day yet and luckily had been chosen for a long afternoon drive, to Sligachan (with a consignment of flowers for the hotel in that grim grey crossroads of valleys beneath the towering mountains) and then on in a north-westerly direction. Bluer and bluer sky as the afternoon wore on, and the sapphire water of sea lochs and streams winding through the rusty heather.

April 25th, Thursday: West Halkin Street

Here I am back in my grey bedroom, making an effort to get to grips with the restless, competitive, jealous, unsatisfied life of this town.

It is the usual problem: I try to straighten my knife and fork and make a neat rectangle in which the meal of my existence is to be swallowed. All yesterday I was busy nibbling at the fringes. I must have a few flowers. Various items of food must be bought. Stamps, the bank. But these are only preparations, painless – or nearly painless – ways of preparing to prepare to face my life. Work: that is the first problem. I must now get down to Desmond's letters, but I would so very much rather have a translation to do.

April 26th

On Wednesday, the day of my return, I watched Princess Alexandra's wedding on Eardley's television, and dined at Magouche's in the evening with the Campbells and Tom Matthews. The Campbells described their Easter at Lambourn with Julia, and how obviously amazed she was with the goings-on of William.[1] From Julia herself yesterday I wasn't surprised to hear that William had been a good deal too much for her: she had never, she declared, been at such close quarters with a small child for so long. We went on to talk about Carrington and her suicide. Last time Julia and I met, Michael Holroyd (who is writing Lytton's life) had just been to see her and she had 'tried to give him some idea of what a remarkable character Carrington was'. I'm not sure how much her present crisis had made her think of the past, nor how much it will be egocentricity on my part to believe she equates Lawrence – Julia – Jenny, with Ralph – Carrington – me. I feel a distaste for putting a special case (and this my own) into the general framework, since each of these cases has its own extraordinary peculiarities. In our 1924–31 situation there was the all-important figure of Lytton, Carrington's devotion to him, the shattering of Ralph's trust in Carrington by the affair with Gerald. Yet I see that *my* view of our joint pasts is not everyone's. As I saw it, when in 1925 the question of Ralph and me going off together arose,

---

[1] Campbell, their son.

Carrington's panic was chiefly lest she should thus lose Lytton. Julia now tells me that Carrington told her that Ralph's withdrawal with me made her fall as it were in love with him again. I believe this may to some extent have been true, though during the four years in which he and I lived in Gordon Square Carrington and Lytton gradually got more and more used to living virtually as a married couple. In her discussion of Carrington's character I sensed in Julia (as I often have before) a very strong ambivalence, references to her genius and remarkable personality being coupled with others to her 'tortured sense of guilt which must have come from deep hostility to others, to her self-confessed masochism, and the strange duplicity and dishonesty of her character. I always thought there was something villainous as well as tragic, something coarse and cruel too, in her face.' Thus she unexpectedly ended her analysis.

Carrington is an emotionally-charged topic for Julia as well as for me, and the charge is different for us both. I'm glad we've broken the long-undisturbed ice over the subject, and hope we shall revert to it.

May 4th: Lambourn

Awoke early from the impact of the deafening country clatter, and was the first down to breakfast at nine. When the others gradually arrived I had read most of the newspaper and was thinking about subjects derived from them: for instance, what are the rules for behaviour concerning Royalty, those dodos whose existence I sometimes deplore, but who are none the less human beings? The function of Royalty is, surely, to smooth over the effects of friction between the countries they symbolize. They shouldn't be used to inflame or express hostility. As I eagerly embarked on what I so love – an argument – I became aware of the reluctance of my companions, Lawrence, Jenny and Julia. Oh dear, yes, I must face the fact that I can't assume that other people like being involved in my favourite pursuit.

162

May 7th: West Halkin Street

I stopped a night with Alix and James at Marlow on the way back to London, enjoyed talking to them enormously but nearly died of the stuffy heat in their house, central heating on full blast, and every window shut and sealed with draughtproof edging and plastic curtains. Every room was almost solid with a stale human smell, and I felt my face grow pillarbox-red. Alix panicked when she found I had opened a tiny window in my room. I wonder what fresh air stands for in psycho-analytical terms? I made an excuse to go out to the garage, so as to breathe in great gouts of the fresh deliciously scented atmosphere. A pure night sky and dark cream three-quarter moon.

May 8th

A train of thought, so I've noticed, once started will rumble along for a week or so, as the undercurrent of my days. My surprised recognition that most people dislike argument is an example. I've asked several people outright whether they do or don't, and the *only* person who has admitted to liking it was Nicko last night. Even Lawrence when asked said, 'No, I like *telling*.' Mary Henderson said, 'No. I like listening.' Yet surely most people would admit to liking thinking, and it's a difficult job to sit down and pursue a train of thought all by oneself. The charm of arguing is that it is thought with the added stimulus given by other people's minds.

May 9th

The texture of my days is getting very densely woven, but the woof and warp have some new threads to them. Work not very important at the moment, but I have just heard that *The President*'s proofs will be here in ten days and they will keep me busy for a bit. Music very dominant. Just as I was thinking of leaving the Hampstead orchestra, they have thrown out a plea for me not to desert. Last night, playing the *Prague* Symphony, was very jolly, and I couldn't imagine being better employed. Afterwards I looked in at Montpelier Square and ate a slice of turkey at Janetta's candlelit table with Robin and Susan Campbell, Magouche and Francis Bacon. Bacon had been drinking since lunch-time, and his

163

curiously pear-shaped face was glistening and blotched with drink as with an infectious disease. The alcoholic 'developer' had brought out his native characteristics of originality and humour. 'Ancient' and 'prehistoric' were the key words of his mood, and he went into a fantastic description of some extraordinary and elaborate stew he had made the evening before for Dicky Chopping – 'It had an *ancient* taste'.

May 14th: Tuesday

Dinner last night with Burgo and Henrietta. Henrietta cooked a delicious meal; Burgo looked bloomingly contented. But having till now shown little signs of her pregnancy, Henrietta suddenly looks weighted and burdened by her child, and my heart goes out to her rather anxiously. The thought of this new being – only a few months off now – kept me restless and wakeful on and off all last night. Today it has rained and rained and I have slid almost unconsciously through the day. A small translation job for Weidenfeld occupies me at the moment.

May 15th: Wednesday

Arthur Waley has just been to lunch with me. Seventy-four, but I must say one wouldn't guess it from the smooth graven oriental mask he presents to the world, and the head well-covered with only partly grey hair. He goes to the British Museum on a bicycle every day and seems wiry and athletic – though rather like Charlie Chaplin seen from the back, with his legs in their baggy trousers under a short tight jacket. It's not this, though, that gives one a hilarious desire to laugh in his august presence – but rather the elaborate air of superiority, the desperately flawless face he presents to the world. Not once did he by word or glance betray the smallest interest in my flat, my pictures, my books, or ask *one single* question about my life. what I was working at, whom I saw. This puts me in a quandary. I must either press on with questions, enquiring into every detail of *his* life and habits, while seeming stingy and ungenerous with information about my own, or volunteer what is obviously not required, and plank down an occasional gobbet – there! take it or leave it. (I havered between the two.) More than once he showed how he values status, prestige, recognition. He talked a lot of Beryl's important role in the dance world, the letters she had had from famous people, the lectures she had given, the articles he was collecting for publication. I suppose he loved her in his way, but it seems as if he loved her reputation even more. He talked about various famous people, or literary friends like Gerald, in a slightly condescending way. He admitted having 'adored' Rupert Brooke at Cambridge, but was eager to tell me how they had both taken their translations of Propertius to their tutor, who said Arthur's was much the best, and how this had made Rupert turn scarlet with rage. What a thing to treasure in your memory!

May 18th, Cambridge

Staying with E.Q. Nicholson.[1] I drove here through the golden afternoon light, striking off from the thunderous clatter of the main road to drift along byroads, through powdery green and blue, lilac and fruit blossom. This little house off Grange Road was Frances Cornford's, and E.Q. has done it up with perfect, pretty and original taste. Yet I was almost overpowered by the very prettiness of my bedroom, with its mauve curtains, white carpets and white French wallpaper splodged with damp-looking violets; and the bosky Cambridge gardens and suburban houses, and above all the Cambridge birds with their deafening chorus (I had the feeling there were thousands of them, HUGE birds sitting in the trees close round the little house). I felt like someone in the illustration of one of Andrew Lang's Fairy Tales, in a curious state of partly beneficent bewitchment, and passed therefore my first night in a state of near-sleeplessness. The strangeness has remained with me through the weekend, but I have shaken down quite happily with it. E.Q's. changeless smile, her gentle, musical voice, her taste, distinction and elegance, her quick responses of liking or disliking (many things – the newspapers – don't exist for her) make up into a baffling personality, and her mind is full of water-tight doors which she pulls down quickly with a smile, as if saying, 'I'm not going to have anything to do with *that*.' Yet she's far from being unsympathetic to human misery and is clearly a kind, loving – if detached – mother.

[1] Elsie Queen (née Myers), widow of Kit, girlhood friend of Rachel Cecil.

Not the least disturbing element of my surroundings was the echo from my Cambridge past, coming like the note of a wind instrument from the heart of a dense, far-off forest, sweet but faint to my inner ear.

Walking with E.Q. along the Backs in their full bloomy spring dress, it was as if I breathed in a heady intoxicating essence from my recollections of May Week balls, the excitement of being young – not in love, but attracted and attracting – of dancing, and kissing in the moonlight. I reacted in a new way too to the delicious prettiness and the lavishness of the college gardens and their good design. One avenue of trees with low spreading branches covered in young yellow-green leaves threw its shade over banks sprinkled with narcissi and scarlet tulips – the effect was ravishing, like an impressionist painting.

The oddest thing I did at Cambridge was to attend a Spiritualist service in the Myers Memorial Hall – an army hut unsuitably erected in memory of E.Q's grandfather, F.W.H. Myers.[1] She knew the 'medium' – a friend having sent her to see E.Q. when she was ill – a kindly looking, very stupid grey-haired middle aged woman. The proceedings were pathetic and absurd. With faces lavender with powder they threw back their heads, closed their eyes and droned out hymn-tunes when the cracked out-of-tune piano struck up. After an 'inspired' address by the medium, we were told: 'She will now connect the two worlds.' She started off at a gallop and in great detail: 'I want to talk to *you* – the lady in the check coat there, I think the gentleman's with you? Well, you're having a bad time about an elderly lady, a lady with white hair sticking out all round her face (accelerando), like a halo. It's a question not exactly of mental disease – but well, yes the trouble *is* mental.' So it went on with vivid personal pictures, and except in about one case the answer would be, '*Yes, yes*, that's right; it's my *mother*.'

What to make of it all? My instinct at the time was that we were witnessing thought-transference. I discussed it with E.Q., who believed it was more than this – clairvoyance, namely power to see what even these people couldn't see! This medium, she said, had correctly foretold the future. I tried to argue with E.Q. that if thought-transference (for which there is evidence) would explain it, one shouldn't make any other assumption – isn't that Occam's

[1]   Well-known spiritualist. Also my father's cousin.

Razor? But she clung to a quiet and obstinate irrationality. It's a curious instance of heredity – first F.W.H. Myers, the highbrow spiritualist, then Leo,[1] who for all his intelligence had a wilful defiant way of embracing irrational beliefs, and now (in the third generation) E.Q.

May 23rd: London

Last night's orchestral dress-rehearsal was purely enjoyable and exciting, but left me with the Beethoven Concerto pounding through my head. Sir Adrian Boult conducted us and Hepzibah Menuhin played the solo part. Boult very genial and youthful, a happy-looking man. The professionalism of both was bracing.

May 28th

My Papacy translation is packed away in its coffin. The proofs of *The President* have come – dare I look at them? When they are finished a little lagoon of calm should stretch ahead.

I had a delightful, peaceful, relaxed weekend alone with Raymond at Crichel – easy and pleasant to the same degree that the last time I was alone with him gave me the feeling *he* at least was not at ease. This augurs well for our Italian trip in September. Talk flowed between us, we picked up our books when we wanted, worked, played croquet and while he took an afternoon nap I walked in summery heat through the quiet woods.

June 1st and 2nd: Stokke

Whitsun weekend looks like being blazingly fine. After Sunday lunch on the lawn in a warm breeze, a talk with Magouche, a walk by myself in the forest and an hour or so correcting my proofs, things and people began to pile up; more and more people telephoned wanting to know if they could come and by evening we were a *horde*, and I was succumbing to my anti-frothblowers' feeling. No, that's not true, I was stimulated by the company and at dinner hooked myself into various nooses of topics with Robin

[1] L.H. Myers, E.Q's father and a great friend of mine, novelist; one-time Marxist.

Fedden, Julian, Tristram Powell and an occasional Magouche. Then there is an uncertain adolescent belt represented by two Fedden girls, Natasha Gorky and a confident blonde friend, and (yet younger) Janetta and Magouche's four little girls. Even this isn't the end – Georgia[1] is expected today and one of Tom Matthews' sons. Heaven knows where they'll all sleep or be, especially if the weather doesn't hold up. It makes fifteen staying in the house, God help us, and the Jellicoes have been asked to lunch. I like to concentrate on my surroundings in detail and depth, not just to let the whirlpool of sound, thoughts and colours rise up and swirl, and then subside leaving pointless lack of recollection. I'd *like* to pay attention to these adolescent girls and discover a little about them – as it is no-one has time for them, they're left to sink or swim. It's as if one were trying to throw up too many juggler's balls. But nearly always a Stokke weekend begins in this way. And why even try to pull shutters down over one's awareness of other people? I can't: they interest me too deeply and agitate me too much. Last night Natasha and Chloe her friend refused to come in to dinner, but sat looking at television. Magouche was furious, and Robin said they 'bloody well ought to be made to'. I felt for their adolescent escapism from the standpoint of my sexagenarian brand of it.

Janetta asked to come to our Medical Orchestra Concert on Friday; I felt she was for once playing the part of my mother or aunt. It was in the great greenish black cavern of the Central Hall, Westminster. But I have enjoyed remembering the whole thing – the curious, rather pathetic excitement and *angst* in the performers' rooms, with the ramifications of responsibility between conductor and orchestra, and the special tension of Hepzibah Menuhin (only Adrian Boult looked and was supremely lackadaisical), the friendliness engendered by this tension, the fact that it 'went' a good deal better than expected from the rehearsals and that our conductor was obviously pleased with us.

The detectable note of an over-loaded plate, and the assault of too great a swarm of bee-sensations has fuzzed the brilliantly fine Whitsun weekend, like a negative taken into the eye of the sun. Nearly all that left its mark on the negative was good in itself, there was just too much of it for me, the oldest by some ten years

[1] Tennant.

of a party which went down through every age-group to Susannah[1] and Rose. I did in the end make touch with the adolescents – the Fedden girls in particular – who responded at once to an invitation to talk about themselves, while Julian and Tristram always have their noses up like fox-terriers to catch any remark that may set off a conversation.

People came and went, there were seventeen to lunch on the lawn on Monday off turkey decorated with buttercups and cowparsley, ham mousse, cold rice salad, aubergines. Lord Shackleton, a Labour peer, turned up to stay the night, as did Tom Matthews' very American son. It was a masterpiece of organization by Magouche (with great support from Janetta) never showing effort, always providing delicious food, and drink; with conversation unflagging and at a high level, with rough croquet and ping-pong and the records of Britten's *War Requiem* (twice played right through and listened to attentively).

Verdict on Britten's Requiem after a fourth hearing: It is a great and moving work and perhaps the most valuable piece of peace propaganda there has been. How much is this due to Owen's marvellous poetry? As I followed the words more closely I saw that Britten had built up the work to a climax where the intense bitterness and sadness (the 'titanic tears' of the earth) stands side by side with the greatest glorification of God. Does he think the two compatible and somehow equatable through the beauty of words and music? But having soaked in the tragic violence of Owen's sonnets, how can one turn to the glory of God, in any sense of 'God'? It's not ironical, that's clear. And if THAT, then how can one accept THIS in the same breath? I suppose it's the same reconciliation that must take place in every true Christian between his worship of the universe and his sense of sin and evil, and how that takes place is something I've not begun to understand.

June 6th: London

Continuing heat-wave. Have just had a picnic lunch with Heywood in Belgrave Square, sitting on a rug in the shadow of an immense

---

[1] Phillips, Magouche's youngest daughter.

black-trunked tree, sipping white wine and eating cold delicacies. It gave me pleasure to profit from the great heat in this way.

But the day began badly. I woke at 4.30, listened for a little to the unearthly hush and then lay for three hours or more staring miserably and anxiously into the blank that is my future. While I am busy I manage to keep the awareness of this dreadful blank in some sense thrust to one side. Though I think of Ralph times without number and in various ways every day (sometimes almost with the same pleased amusement and vividness as if he were alive) I contrive *not to face* his absence fairly and squarely. But as soon as the pressure of work or people eases off, back rushes the tidal wave of longing and loneliness and pain, almost unchanged since the very first. I stand like a sombre black rock while it washes and swirls over me, unable to do anything but just endure and wait. This is what happened this morning, and I was full of wonder at the self-deception which had made me seem (as I suppose) to others to be making a go of my life. This morning I felt myself drowning in envy for everyone who had someone to be responsible for, to be responsible for them, to discuss their worries and minute daily experiences with; to go and lean on in moments of weakness, huddle up to for blessed animal warmth, to love and be loved by. Oh, what endless courage one has to keep stoking up to walk one's cold frightening path alone!

The President went off only yesterday – but the day before Dermod came to dinner and instead of this being an encouragement to me to go back to Desmond's letters, it's done just the opposite – made me decide they must definitely be abandoned. He has veered right round as a result of a visit from Michael, and now shares his view that it is 'too soon'. When I said that I was convinced we'd better give it all up he protested, but I'm sure he was relieved. He talks of wanting to avoid the 'sensational' as if any of Desmond's letters were *that*! Obviously even those to Cynthia Asquith would have been censored by the family. No; it's impossible – and I have few regrets. If I had another book to translate I should have none. He asked me if I thought Desmond 'would have minded' publication, and I searched the inside of my head and said truthfully that I thought he would have liked the idea of being faithfully presented to posterity.

June 10th

Everyone talks excitedly about the great Profumo scandal, which may even bring the Conservative party toppling. It was argued at Robert's and also with Janetta, Magouche, Robin Fedden, and Gamel (just arrived from Spain) in Montpelier Square. Because the *only* serious casualty is likely to be the Conservative Party everyone is very light-hearted about it.

Robert's mother was indignant about Mr Profumo – 'He ought to have been castigated at birth!' she said.

June 11th

Last night I dined with Magouche, her two Gorky daughters, Eduardo Paolozzi and a successful painter called Kitaj. Magouche has a stained-glass glow about her which heartens one, and looked really beautiful in a clotted-cream wool dress with thick bright blue beads. We sat out on her terrace then indoors talking – talk borne along on two rival streams: one was Eduardo's curious, very personal brand of naive thoughtfulness. His censor lets everything through, opening the door with a wide respectful gesture to the simplest, most well-worn of notions, which are ushered in as if they were exotic and original inspirations – such was that 'really the Conservative Party are behind the times'. The other was Kitaj's compulsive and fanatical Marxism. He was expecting to find a defence of class distinctions in Magouche and me, and clearly disconcerted somewhat by the ground being hacked away under his feet when I quickly handed him the monarchy, religion, the House of Lords and the public schools. Did he believe in reality of progress? Magouche asked. 'Yes, *absolutely*,' and his closely furred face, so reminiscent of Van Gogh, crunched up with badger-like rebarbativeness and aggression. He is not at all a stupid man, however, and interesting though not entirely likeable.

I've had a letter from Dermod taking it all back. What's to be made of that?

June 12th

Unreal effect of living in this permanent Mediterranean radiance. A fillip given by my being offered a job yesterday by Weidenfeld, to translate a short art book from the French – and also by being with people I greatly like or love. Janetta suddenly was at my door, looking fresh as a daisy in a pink suit and carrying a bunch of rosebuds.

A series of early-morning telephone calls from Julia. Yes, she and Lawrence would come to dinner; she wanted to know at what time. 'About this dinner party . . .' F: (exasperated) 'It's *not* a dinner-party, Julia, just old friends eating together. I've not asked another soul and won't if you like.' Then as it so happened, Robin Campbell rang up, full of friendliness and having left his family in Wales. I therefore had to telephone Julia and persuade her that this didn't make it a dinner-party – it was difficult, because I already heard her drawing herself up into her 'social occasion' position. Lastly, about five-thirty she rang up with 'bad news'; her temperature was 'just over 99 and she thought she shouldn't go out'. Well, at the end of this series of calls I was luckily able to get the Godleys to come and eat the delicious piece of salmon I'd already cooked for dinner and we had a very nice evening.

Today I lunched with Frances Phipps, who was rejoicing because Kennedy has made a speech *in favour of peace*. How astonishing that this should seem a surprising event. Yet it does, and is the most politically encouraging thing that has happened for years. He's actually tried to sell peace to the Americans, and spoken well and feelingly, without clichés – 'I speak of peace, as the necessary, rational end of rational men. Too many of us think it impossible. We need not accept that view. Our problems are man-made – therefore they can be solved by man.'

June 20th: Thursday

There has been a longish gap since I last wrote, and in this case 'No news is good news'. I have the feeling that I have lately been 'riding' my life, rather than it riding me. One reason it has been more 'in hand' lately, responding to bit or brake, is that I've become so deeply immersed in other people's affairs. I've had two delightful visits from Janetta, who was beset with problems.

There has also been a very strange sequel to my visit to the Cambridge séance. E.Q. came to lunch a few days ago, and I asked her if she'd heard any more from the medium. 'Yes, she wrote to me, and said she was afraid she had been off form, and not doing well at all. She said she saw someone connected with you or me, she wasn't sure which.' 'Oh, what were they like?' 'It was a young man who had been up at Cambridge, and had very fair hair. And as Tim is as dark as Burgo I thought she'd got it wrong.' I began to search my mind and thought naturally of Julian, but said nothing. Then E.Q. said in her very quiet gentle voice which makes everything more telling: 'She said his name was *Julian*.'

I was fairly flummoxed. I was *almost convinced* that while I was enjoying the high comedy and interest of it all I *did* think of Julian, and that it would amuse me (and perhaps him) if I described it all to him when I next saw him, soon afterwards. If this is so, it backs up my belief that I witnessed genuine telepathy that evening.

I had Eardley and Frances Phipps to an unplannned lunch yesterday; my halibut baked with onions, mushrooms and bacon was a success, and the conversation was real, full of ideas strung through (as beads on a necklace) by the fact that we all liked each other. After Eardley left, Frances stayed on telling me about a dinnerparty which had 'not been a success, mainly because Raymond had failed to connect'. She asked Paul[1] if he could throw light on this, and with a broad grin he said it was because he had been given no whiskey after dinner (only superb wines at dinner and cherry brandy afterwards) and 'if you have important people to dinner, etc.' I felt for Frances, or with her, when she said: 'But I don't want Raymond to come *because he's an important person*, only because he's a friend.' She was wounded and couldn't quite detect the source of her pain – I think it was that her hospitality should have been taken in such a materialistic way.

June 30th: Charleston

A wet but happy weekend. Now the sun has come out (on Sunday afternoon) and shines down heavily from between the clouds onto the wet sweet-smelling garden, bringing a lot of flies buzzing everywhere. The steamy air smells of manure and roses. I'm sitting alone on a long bench which looks like something for carrying coffins to the grave, in the clumsy but charming paved garden made by Quentin. A little basin of duckweed-covered water edged with his home-made tiles, columbines sprouting from between the mosaics

---

[1] Hyslop, friend of Raymond's.

in the pavement that the frosts have left intact. This time I'm entirely captivated by the Charleston ambience and feel its civilization rather than its ramshackleness. At every turn Barbara tugs the conversation back to herself, or her children or the eminent Bloomsburies she likes to feel she was so very close to. I have heard many stories for the fifth or sixth time – the one about the Musk Orchid for about the tenth – but I was asking for this when I brought back Butterfly Orchids from the wood at the end of the drive. Yesterday I climbed in a strong wind and sprinkling rain to the top of the downs, collecting any flowers I liked the look of, like shells on a beach, and on the lowest slope came to a great plantation of Fragrant and Spotted Orchids. I've really been happy here; Clive and Duncan both in splendid form. A very interesting conversation on ambiguity prompted by listening to *Pelléas and Mélisande*, which scoured the edges of a fascinating subject without clearing the middle. What is the pleasure one gets from ambiguity, or lack of definition, such as that opera arouses? Duncan thought it thrilling, in a way that nothing completely defined and exact can be. I feel a reservation, doubts. For a thing to have two – or even several – meanings may give a complicated and interesting result. But for it to end in a fog of uncertainty which is never resolved, somehow leaves me frustrated and feeling swindled. Do I miss something? *Why* should imprecision as such be thrilling? Something to go on pondering about.

Clive asked me at tea whether I thought my character had changed much in the last twenty years – because, he went on, he though I had become more 'active'.

July 5th: London

I have been immersed in old letters and found it disturbing. I swing between over- and under-estimation, in the course of which a lot goes into the waste-paper basket. Ralph had the theory that 'everything must be kept'. I know that simply leads in the end to total destruction, and there's something melancholy in the thought of all these tin boxes, full of tied-up letters, such as I saw at Charleston.

Last night I sat for about three hours reading my own letters to Ralph and throwing away quite a lot. I woke at five this morning and went on with it, although finding deep sadness in this stale dry dust emanating from the rich and living years. As our lives became bound together and the time came when we were virtually never apart there was hardly ever an occasion for writing, and I have the feeling that pen and paper was an unsuitable vehicle for intimacy and love that expressed itself so completely and so easily in conversation and caresses.

July 7th: Cranborne

I came to Cranborne early yesterday, and now it's Sunday morning, and I sit on the lawn of this sympathetic house. The rain has brought down a carpet of rose petals and behind me hangs a magnificent syringa like a white curtain. Otherwise the garden is shaggy, flowerless and neglected. What do I particularly like about the conversation in this house? Generalizations sprout in it like mushrooms. Even Laura, who brought a schoolfriend over yesterday afternoon, is fertile in them – strange, perhaps unsound, but stimulating ones based generally on human behaviour. Human behaviour is the material of much of the talk (and this I also enjoy).

July 11th: London

I feel sometimes like a waiter compelled to go round a room crowded with people, holding out a tray on which they put their empty cups and glasses of ideas. The Cecil family are delightfully free with theirs, and slap them down without waiting to be asked, but sometimes I look in surprise at what my tray has collected and can't make head or tail of it. Some of Hugh's contributions, freely given though they were, seemed to startle even himself. Laura will come to a sweeping conclusion about human nature beginning, 'I've always noticed', and is amazed because nobody else has.

Yesterday I had a delightful evening with Eardley, dining and talking hard. (Did I talk most or hold the tray? The tray, I think.) And afterwards we went to a party at the Tate for a retrospective show of Ivon Hitchens' paintings – a huge concourse of art lovers in evening dress, moving dreamily about among candles. Not a face I knew, save Cressida Ridley's. The paintings were perhaps too much alike, but if only the best had been on show one would have admired their soft richness, their gentle and persuasive quality. One sank into them like well-upholstered chairs.

175

Whenever dire need of support comes over me my mind flies to Janetta. Who else, young though she is, and also so leant upon and weighed down by everyone? I know that her great kindness and responsibility would make her always come in answer to a direct and urgent appeal, but that's the one thing I don't want to add to her difficulties by making if I can help it, and I'm very far from that situation at the moment. Yesterday we arranged to spend the evening together tonight, but from this morning's conversation I rather think she's forgotten it. Robin is dining with her, and I dread so much to press in when not wanted that I didn't say to her, 'We were going to have this evening, do you remember?'

Later: After a quiet working day and a nice tea-time visit from Frances Phipps, bringing me a rose and a plumbago in two pots, I remained in indecision until Janetta rang up at eight and asked me to join her and Robin, and we spent the evening as I most love spending evenings, domestically and effortlessly, talking (three is a good number), eating simply, doing a little mending. Robin has had a second son. Talking about this and his adored William I glanced back into the long-closed world of parenthood to young children, with all its warmth and interest, happiness and anguish. Robin loves William like a mother rather than a father, entering into all his feelings painfully, following him with anxious eyes as he trots into school, dragging his satchel. As he said unforgettably: 'There's nothing in the world worse than seeing one's nipper trying to be brave.'

July 18th

Took Julian and the Jenkinses to *Oh, What a Lovely War!* They were enthusiastic; I couldn't feel the same. Was it because it seemed to do no more than twang on an old tired nerve? Or was it that the play is trying to shock people into a view that I've held so long that I had no further response to make to it? Or that its thesis – that war is unspeakably ghastly and the 1914–18 war was far the worst of all – is something I feel more deeply and painfully than anything else, so that this rather slick, deft, vulgar trifle didn't seem to go far enough for me? I was groping about for the reason of my lack of reaction (not a tear, not a genuine irresistible laugh) as we strolled through Leicester Square, when Julian mentioned

Owen's poems as if they were comparable with the diaries and songs (genuine material though these were) quoted in this revue. This gave me a sharp, quite violent shock, for Owen's poems hit the nail right on the head, and never make the slightest error of taste. To mention them in the same breath as this cheap, well-meaning, trumpery affair seemed strange.

July 19th

I lunched alone with Janetta and Robert, which brought a great wave of nostalgia for the impossible back again. Yes, even now. It delighted me to find Janetta in total agreement with me about *Oh, What a Lovely War!*, but better at analysing the reason for her reaction than I, or possibly not having such cause to suspect personal reasons. Robert stuck up for it but not aggressively and put his case well. He thought it of particular importance that it was the work of the young who had experienced nothing and probably read little about the 1914–18 war, so that their reaction of horror was genuine and fresh and peculiarly their own, and he found it deeply moving.

August 1st

How I wish this baby would arrive! These last days have been coloured by sympathetic feelings for Burgo and Henrietta, full of anxious empathy, a sense of responsibility, and self-questioning how to support without interfering or fussing.

I heard with considerable agitation that Angelica, Bunny and the twins had all gone off to France with no prospect of returning for weeks. What is to be made of this seeming desertion which leaves me especially anxious not to do likewise? I was reassured by a telephone conversation with Henrietta's doctor last night an hour after he'd seen her. She was 'fine', everything was absolutely normal, and if the baby is not here by next Wednesday they will 'induce' it, and put a term to their waiting. I think of them and their child and its future endlessly, and feel as restless as a cat.

Bank Holiday Monday

Arrived at Halkin Street after a Stokke weekend with mixed feelings. It is my own. I can do absolutely what I like in it – but that means that I must develop a desire, an impulse at least and force myself to carry it out. Otherwise disintegration. I rang Burgo and Henrietta, who seemed pleased at the idea of coming to have a picnic supper with me, and the evening passed pleasantly away. I drove them home soon after ten-thirty, and about an hour later when I was settling into bed the telephone rang. It was Burgo, saying that Henrietta's hands and ankles had swollen and she had an irritating rash. Now was my chance to be some use. I went round to their flat and my first impression was that nothing much was wrong. Poor Henrietta lay on the tumbled bed, managing to look very pretty though so heavily laden, in her simple white nightgown. The swelling was not acute; she had a definite sort of nettle-rash though, and she was afraid, from a book she'd read, she had toxaemia. I sat talking to them until at last a little sandy locum tenens arrived and examined her thoroughly. All other doctors connected with her were away on this mad festive beano. Talked to Burgo in the sitting-room where I saw the touching sight of a tiny half-knitted pink garment lying on the collapsing sofa. The doctor announced that she *had* toxaemia, and sent for the ambulance. In a surprisingly short time a dark-blue-clad officer had arrived and she had gone down in her nightie and a thin dressing-gown, and Burgo too, to face her fate. What courage it needs – yet almost every female faces it. Burgo didn't return, so I realized he'd gone in the ambulance and took myself off.

It is six o'clock on Tuesday and I've heard nothing except a call from Burgo this morning to say the doctors at the hospital said it was not toxaemia but some sort of allergy. However they are keeping her and I hope it will be 'induced' today or tomorrow.

August 7th: Wednesday

Nine o'clock in the morning – the sky has again become a sheet of purest blue, and the pigeons sit in a row on the roof looking in at me. Yesterday passed in unnatural calm. The fact that Henrietta is in professional and skilled hands is a great relief. Knowing that the 'inducing' might not start until today I restrained myself from

178

ringing up and heard nothing till Burgo came in the evening, having been to see her. I've just rung up the hospital and heard Henrietta's voice saying quite jubilantly, 'I've started to have it.' Thank heavens for that! It shouldn't be too long now.

August 8th, Thursday

Very perturbed by calling the hospital and being told 'no change'. Last night Burgo thought the child should have been there already. He had been with Henrietta during the afternoon when 'contractions were coming every five minutes', but I feel he has no real conception of how much more tremendous the whole process had to become. I spent most of yesterday, and am today, in the middle of a familiar frantic attempt to wait calmly.

3 p.m. I'm seriously worried. Rang Henrietta's doctor at lunchtime and he broached the possibility of a Caesarian if nothing has happened by tomorrow morning. 'I don't understand it,' he said, 'she's so young, everything's normal, and she does everything she's told.' Yet she is having contractions, but no more. My heart bleeds for her, and I don't know how to get through the time.

9.30 p.m. I had E.Q. to supper but it was a *supplice*. Would it have been more so to be alone? I don't know. Burgo came in for a drink; he had been told about the possible Caesarian and was dreadfully shaken. Duncan rang up and it was some small consolation to talk to someone who also really cared about that sweet girl. I feel like someone caught in the wreck of a railway accident.

August 14th

The gap is the measure of how long it took me to recover from catapulting so hopelessly into agitation. Henrietta and Burgo's dear little baby, Sophie Vanessa, is now five days old and Henrietta is recovering from the operation. Their delight in their child is marvellous to see and they express it with refreshing abandon. I have been twice to see Henrietta and had Burgo here a good many times – hoping not to seem interfering or fussing, but now sure that attentions and interest are appreciated. I have been much moved – obsessed is really the word – by the whole thing. Each night as I close my eyes to the darkness this obsession returns, even if it has been quiescent all day. The baby looks very like Henrietta, with a wide mouth and perfect little hands.

August 16th

I've been all day on the run – to see Craig in the morning – to visit Henrietta in the afternoon – a drink with Isobel in the evening. I feel like one of the silver balls in machines in fairs, which gets shot up by the insertion of a penny, bounces wildly from metal peg to metal peg, rattles here, slides along there, jingles and jolts until it drops into the last hole of all from which there is no return. Henrietta comes out of hospital on Friday, and after buying her a pram with Burgo and driving her home – what then? It's difficult to strike a happy balance between doing all one can, and longs to do for those one loves, and backing gracefully off the stage. I see clearly the warning Ralph would have been the first to give me: don't interfere in their lives. But I'm aware of one thing at least: here at last, in flesh and blood, is a motive for going on far stronger than any I have encountered during nearly three years of struggle.

Index

186